TABLE OF CONTENTS

PART THREE: THE QUALITY PROPOSAL

PART FOUR: THE CHALLENGE

APPENDIX A

"I commend you for your terrific work. This book is something of real value. It is also something I have not seen before ... the materials on quality in proposal writing are standard setting. It is easy to say, everyone who writes proposals needs this book. It provides a clear view of the proposal's purpose in the sales process and how to develop the right one for each situation. It is filled with new ideas that I intend to use in our proposals."

Bill Evans
The Evans Group

"[This book] cuts through the 'hype' associated with sales training and provides a no-nonsense, professional guide to the sales process and proposal writing. Concepts like 'The empty suit syndrome,' 'Go with what you've got,' and 'The Seven Deadly Mistakes,' show the depth and experience from which this book is born. Kantin and Hardwick hit the nail on the head and make a valuable contribution to the selling profession."

Ronald R. Evans
Senior Manager, *Ernst & Young*

"... a useful, insightful book worth owning as a business tool. Competition intensifying makes this book a must read... quality proposals do sell business."

Michael S. Schwartz
President, *Synapse Human Resource Consulting Group*

"During my review of the book, I was completing three major proposals– I rewrote all three. Any sales professional or consultant will appreciate the depth and thoroughness of this book. It certainly will become my handbook and reference for future proposals."

Al Alcala
President, *Byte Images Inc.*

"This book shows that the authors have been on both sides of the sales desk. Their practical and useful examples can be applied for the benefit of the customer and the sales person. The "strawman proposal" tips are excellent tools anchored within an indispensable, practical, and simple sales system. This book focuses on the lost principles of identifying and serving customer needs."

Glen R. Gross
Director of Management Development & Training, *Barnett Ban*

"Quality tips and tools, not theory. This book takes quality processes to the next step—application to the sales function. This book should become the educational guide for sales professionals looking for success in the 90s."

Russell L. Fluery
Performance Dynamics

"This is the most insightful book I have read on selling; it provides practical models, systems, examples, and tangibles, instead of the typical theories and gimmicks. I think Kantin and Hardwick have astutely linked sales, quality service, and proposals into a winning combination. This is the kind of book that should be required reading for any business school student planning a career in marketing or sales; it's reality-based."

Darrell L. Ward, Ph. D.
President and CEO, *HyperGraphics*

"A salient contribution of the book is promoting an awareness of the need for customer-based, systematic proposals in the sales cycle. My experience in the sales arena strongly suggests that a large number of buying situations call for formal proposals. Unfortunately, it is the exception for a proposal to appear, and in the rare instance, the product too often is of 'boiler-plate' variety.

This book also offers a timely, leadership guide for sales managers looking to create a more competitive and quality focus for their sales organization. It should become a training tool and reference for sales professionals and consultants. I look forward to reviewing the authors' proposal writing seminar and workbook."

Richard W. Hansen, Ph.D.
Professor of Marketing, Southern Methodist University
Edwin L. Cox School of Business

QUALITY SELLING THROUGH QUALITY PROPOSALS

◆

A NO-NONSENSE GUIDE TO DEVELOPING WINNING SALES PARTNERSHIPS

Robert F. Kantin
&
Mark W. Hardwick, Ph. D.

bf

boyd & fraser publishing company

The Scientific Press Series

Copyright 1994 by boyd & fraser publishing company
A Division of South-Western Publishing Company
One Corporate Place • Ferncroft Village
Danvers, Massachusetts 01923

International Thomson Publishing
I(T)P boyd & fraser publishing company is an ITP Company.
The ITP trademark is used under license.

All rights reserved. No part of this work may be reproduced or used in any form or by any means—graphic, electronic, or mechanical, including photo-copying, recording, taping, or information or retrieval systems—without permission in writing from the publisher.

Names of all products mentioned herein are used for identification purposes only and may be trademarks and/or registered trademarks of their respective owners. South-Western Publishing Company and boyd & fraser publishing company disclaim any affiliation, association, or connection with, or sponsor-ship or endorsement by such owners.

Manufactured in the United States of America

ISBN: 0-89426-224-6
Stock Number: SP2246

1 2 3 4 5 6 7 8 9 10 BW 9 8 7 6 5 4

ACKNOWLEDGEMENTS

This book represents the culmination of experience, research, hard work, and the encouragement of many people. Thanks to Helen Hardwick for editing, proofreading, and making this book more readable. We also want to thank our friends and colleagues for their valuable comments, ideas, contributions, and criticisms — they were all generous with their time and suggestions. Thanks to Bill Evans, Bob Heckman, Ron Evans, Dick Hansen, Michael Schwartz, C. Patrick Hardwick, Glen Gross, Russ Fluery and Darrell Ward. Special thanks to Jeff Hardwick who helped us understand the mysteries and magic of the publishing business.

To
Marylee,
Helen, Jeff, Brian & Todd

our sources of support, encouragement, and love.

EXHIBITS

"Quality improvement techniques represent a whole new way of doing business... If customers are the people who receive your work, only they can determine what quality is, only they can tell you what they want and how they want it. That's why a popular slogan of the quality movement is "quality begins with the customer."

Peter Scholtes
The Team Handbook
(Joiner Associates, Inc., 1990)

FOREWORD

In today's competitive world, most prospective customers want to "see it in writing" prior to making the buy decision. There is simply too much at stake for the buyer to take a chance on anything less than the best possible solution.

This presents a major challenge to sales professionals and consultants ... translating weeks, and in many cases, months of sales activity, plus lots of hard work and expense into a written proposal. In other words, all of the planning, rapport building, sales calls, product presentations, references and related activities will be reduced to a 8-1/2" x 11" document.

Can your organization take a chance on an inferior, or even an 'average' proposal and jeopardize the overall success of the sales mission?

A visit to your local library or neighborhood bookstore will reveal numerous books and articles on selling, customer service, and quality. However, there is a noticeable absence of books on the subject of creating a "quality proposal". In their book, *Quality Selling Through Quality Proposals*, Bob Kantin and Mark Hardwick view the creation of a customer-driven proposal as a vital link in the sales process. They advance the theory that quality standards must be applied to selling and writing proposals, just as they have been applied to customer service and manufacturing. A unique concept the authors present, is that sales activities represent the first opportunity an organization has to provide quality service to a prospective customer. This book also proposes that a written proposal is the first product an organization delivers to a customer.

While the subject of quality and customer service is a more recent phenomenon, having reached a fever pitch in just the last few years, the subject of selling has been written about for decades. But, the integration of quality in the selling process has not been broached until this book.

Students of selling and marketing read thousands of books, attend hundreds of sales rallies and conventions, and buy millions of dollars worth of audio and video tapes to basically achieve one objective — selling more effectively. The subject of proposal writing receives cursory mention in the vast majority of published information on selling. Everyone feels that it is important and stresses the need, but does not provide a clear-cut methodology for organizing and completing the mission.

Almost 10 years ago, quality and customer service received a shot in the arm in the form of the book, *In Search of Excellence*. This instant best seller described the way excellent companies approached their respective market places and emphasized the need for quality and genuine concern for customer service. *Quality Selling Through Quality Proposals* brings together the selling process and the need to continuously strive for quality. Based upon first-hand experiences, the authors present a sophisticated but basic sales process, analyze the purpose of a proposal, and create a road map which can provide even the most experienced sales professional with a template and methodology that makes business sense.

This book not only shows the reader how to organize for the proposal effort, but how to apply the "Quality Proposal RATER" in evaluating their own proposals and those of their competitors. This proposal rating instrument becomes a tool, not only to help measure quality in proposals, but to debrief a prospective client after a win or loss in a competitive situation. This important element of seeing your proposal "through the customer's eyes" provides new insight into the entire sales process. It should result in more effective and successful proposals.

This book provides the essential elements, structures, and substantive examples for quality selling and writing quality proposals. The authors provide the necessary "How To" rather than pontificating and talking in generalities ... the problem with so many books on selling, customer service, and quality.

With the emphasis on an organization being both market and customer-driven, doesn't it make sense to apply quality principles to the most critical sales document — the proposal?

Within Andersen Consulting, an important concept in preparing to meet with a prospective client is to fully understand that client's "BUYER VALUES." In other words, determining what's important to the prospective client and demonstrating how our services and products meet and exceed those requirements. The key "BUYER VALUE" behind *Quality Selling Through Quality Proposals* is the years of experience incorporated into the authors' approach and the book's many useful examples, team methodologies, audit questionnaire, sales letters, and diagrams. This book's concepts can be used in virtually any business which calls for a formal proposal as part of doing business. This book works!

Robert A. Heckman
Andersen Consulting

INTRODUCTION

The Complex Sale

This book is intended for sales professionals and consultants whose success depends upon making 'complex sales'. A complex sale meets one or more of the following criteria:

* the proposed service or product provides a sophisticated or innovative business approach for the buyer
* the proposed service's or product's financial and non-financial benefits are not readily apparent
* buying approvals must come from more than one individual or one level of the buyer's organization
* the selling organization's proposed service or product solves a complicated business problem for the buyer
* the selling organization employs team selling techniques with the buyer

Further, this book is intended for sales professionals and consultants who use or want to use proposals as an integral part of their selling process.

Reasons for Writing This Book

The original idea for writing this book came to us after we completed a large proposal for a friend's company. Our friend was impressed with what we considered to be a typical business proposal. We thought everyone's proposals followed basic structure and format standards — standards for content, flow, required information, and appearance. After doing some research and reviewing scores of business proposals from companies in different industries, we realized there were no standards.

Our research also included a review of many books available on selling. Some of these books suggested or recommended salespeople write proposals, but few devoted more than one or two pages to the topic; none provided guidelines. Rather, most of the sales books focused on various selling processes and others unveiled the latest sales fads and gimmicks. Only a few books pierced the concept of "walking the talk" — helping a buyer to buy by documenting how the proposed service or product would make or save money. None of the sales books discussed the interdependence of effective sales processes and writing a quality proposal.

Quality as a Major Theme

By coincidence, while we began to work on this book, we also started a consulting engagement on quality customer service. Our research led us to some of the current books and articles on the quality movement underway in this country. We highly recommend the following books:

- *Delivering Quality Service* by Zeithaml, Parasuraman, and Berry
- *Out of the Crisis* by Deming
- *The Team Handbook* by Scholtes

The major themes in these books are, quality:

- improvement requires visionary and enlightened leadership — done through empowerment of employees
- is everyone's business no matter what department or function — it's a team approach
- improvement is not a quick fix, it lasts forever — it's a process, not a program
- is customer-driven or customer-focused — not focused on the organization's profit goals

In researching the quality movement, we also realized that sales functions receive little, if any, time under the quality assurance microscope. Some of the reasons for this oversight may stem from the movement's primary focus on production and customer service. We think sales has been overlooked as the first opportunity any organization has to demonstrate quality service to a potential customer.

Interrelationships: Quality, Sales, and Proposals

As we expanded our knowledge on quality and got deeper into writing this book, we identified and defined the interrelationships between selling activities, written proposals, and quality service. We soon concluded that we needed to expand the book's scope to include a:

* basic sales system with structured activities and processes for developing a quality, written proposal
* clear focus on quality in selling: all sales activities and processes must be buyer-driven — based on each buyer's unique needs and wants

Experiences and Observations

As we wrote this book, we reflected on our experiences as entrepreneurs in a consulting and professional services business. Our first year's revenues were over a $1.2 million dollars with pre-tax margins of 22%. We attributed much of our sales successes to our buyer-driven proposals. We also realized most of our selling failures often resulted from not following our then unwritten sales and quality proposal guidelines.

We also reflected on our experiences and frustrations with the sales processes of several software and service companies. Some of these companies placed an over-reliance on results and failed miserably to provide effective processes, systems, and training to help their sales-people get those results. Others over-emphasized the need to develop social relationships with their buyers rather than provide them with business solutions. Some failed to educate their salespeople not only on their services or products but, more importantly, on how to use them to solve a buyer's business problem. It was not surprising that some of these companies had more concern for their corporate needs and wants than for the proposition of "Customer First".

More About This Book

This book applies the practical principles of quality service to sales. It defines some practical steps and guidelines for selling and writing proposals. These steps or guidelines will not make selling or proposal writing any easier; however, they will remove some of the mystery, fear, and intimidation from these activities.

After writing this book, we think one critical, unanswered question remains:

Are senior management and sales professionals willing or ready to admit quality improvements are needed in the complex sale?

"It takes courage to admit that you have been doing something wrong, to admit you have something to learn, that there is a better way."

Dr. W. Edwards Deming
Out of the Crisis, 10th Printing
Massachusetts Institute of Technology, August 1990

RECOMMENDATIONS AND COMMENTS BEFORE READING

Recommendations for Different Reader Categories

We expect three broad categories of people with various levels of experience and training will read this book:

- consultants with no formal sales training
- inexperienced sales professionals with limited sales training
- experienced sales professionals and managers with various levels and types of sales training

Recommendations for Consultants and Inexperienced Sales Professionals

We think consultants and inexperienced sales professionals will benefit from reading this book by gaining insight and knowledge of:

- a customer-driven sales process
- a basic, structured sales system
- techniques and guidelines for writing sales proposals

We think this book will become a reference for their future selling and proposal writing activities.

Recommendations for Experienced Sales Professionals and Managers

We think experienced sales professionals and sales managers know the benefit of grounding and aligning sales activities in a structured sales system. We also think they may not want to read about our sales system.

However, we do recommend they:

- read *Chapter 1* to get an understanding of our concern for **putting quality in sales**
- examine *Chapter 4* which contains a **buyer audit questionnaire**
- review the **"Confirmation Letter"** and **"Pre-proposal Letter"** in *Chapters 4 and 5.*

After reviewing these three areas, experienced sales professionals and managers might want to begin reading Chapter 6. After reading this book, we think they will use this book as a reference for writing and rating the quality of their proposals.

Comments on Format, Organization, and Content

Before writing this book, we researched literature and studies on how people read, process, and remember information and use books as references. Because most books are written in standard paragraph format, they force readers to underline or highlight important points to organize and assimilate information. To enhance the readability and utility of this book, we wrote so readers can:

- comprehend the information easily and quickly
- easily scan and find information without having to read or reread an entire chapter
- improve the effectiveness and efficiency of reading by reducing the amount of analysis needed to determine the relevance and importance of the information presented

From our research and past experiences, we also realize adults learn by examples. Therefore, the book contains examples and models of letters, questionnaires, proposal sections and subsections, and a complete quality proposal example. We think these examples will facilitate the learning process and provide practical, no-nonsense tools for selling and writing quality proposals.

CHAPTER 1

QUALITY PROPOSALS:
THE MISSING LINK IN SALES PARTNERSHIPS

Quality Defined

Quality, you will know it when you feel or experience it.

What have others said about quality?

W. Edwards Deming, the internationally renowned consultant who led the Japanese into new principles of management, productivity and quality, states:

> *"Quality consists of the capacity to satisfy wants..."*

Stew Leonard, President of Stew Leonard's food store, on quality:

> *"Customers define it, and employees provide it ...*
> *Rule #1: The customer is always right!*
> *Rule #2: If you think the customer is ever wrong, reread Rule #1!"*

Michael Spiess, Vice President of The Wallace Co., a Malcolm Baldrige National Quality Award winner, says,

> *"Our belief is that quality issues drive business issues, that they're really not separate at all. We believe that the better we get at meeting customers' expectations, the better our business will become. Statistically, that has proven to be the case."*

Steve Jobs, Founder of Apple Computer, on quality:

"Be a yard stick of quality. Some people are not use to an environment where excellence is expected."

D. J. DePree, Founder of Herman Miller, Inc. said,

"Quality is a matter of truth."

His son, Max DePree, Chairman and CEO of Herman Miller Inc. says,

"When we talk about quality, we are talking about quality of product and service ... but [we are] also talking about the quality of our relationships and the quality of our communications and the quality of our promises to each other. And so it is reasonable to think about quality in terms of truth and integrity."

Some experts call quality the "Big Q" as Larry Wilson, Founder of Wilson Learning, a national sales training company, says,

"At Wilson Learning, when we talk about quality ... we are not only talking about statistical quality control or quality control personnel. We ... call "Big Q" quality a corporate culture that promotes, protects, and champions quality at every level of the organization, from the board of directors, to sales, to the warehouse ... quality means every individual throughout the organization being committed to doing what's right."

In their book *In Search of Excellence*, Thomas J. Peters and Robert H. Watterman, define quality:

"There is nothing like quality. It is the most important word used ... Quality leads to a focus on innovativeness — to doing the best one can for every customer on every product; hence it is a goad to productivity, automatic excitement, an external focus. The drive to make "the best" affects virtually every function of the organization."

What Happened to Quality Selling?

In the past, it seems there was less hype and more intimacy in selling. Quality sales meant working with buyers to help them make buying decisions. Unfortunately, some of today's sales leaders have lost the vision for quality. They have replaced quality selling activities with "efforting," self-interests, and superficial programs. This type of leadership prescribes:

- doing what has been done before but doing it 5% or 10% better
- quick fixes and magic sales pills
- top-down sales forecasting done in a vacuum
- short-term thinking—hitting the monthly or quarterly numbers
- making more calls as the only means to making quota

These sales organizations do not understand quality selling. They place their needs before those of their customers. They have a "let's try to sell them something" approach rather than trying to present buyers with viable business solutions. They discount the need to first understand the buyer's business before trying to sell. These sales organizations do not understand that the world and buyers' expectations have changed.

Quality in Sales — A Partnership

What does quality in the sales function mean? It means exceeding the promises made to customers or backing the promises of sales. It means "walking the talk" by showing a buyer how the proposed service or product will save or make them money. It means forming a *partnership* between the buyer and the seller.

At the organization level, quality selling includes the development of a sales system that promotes excellence. The organization must anchor its sales system in *partnering* processes that support the:

- establishment of ongoing positive relationships and communications
- development of a clear understanding of a buyer's business

- identification and confirmation of the buyer's needs and wants
- presentation of viable business alternatives for solving business problems or capitalizing on business opportunities

A sales partnership always creates a win-win situation for the buyer and the seller.

On the individual level, quality selling means treating the buyer like a business *partner* not an opponent. Quality selling is collaborative, consultative, and cooperative. A sales professional never manipulates the buyer into buying. Quality selling means the sales professional:

- goes the extra mile to do what is right
- meets or exceeds the buyer's expectations
- builds trust through honesty and integrity in all sales activities

Quality selling means customer-driven partnerships not sales-driven programs.

The Missing Link

Quality sales proposals are the single-most neglected element or "missing link" in sales partnerships. In many partnerships, a sales professional may need to spend weeks or even months trying to understand the buyer's business and to define viable business solutions for a buyer's problem or opportunity. The buyer and the seller make an investment of time and money in the partnership. Ironically, just as the partnership reaches an obvious conclusion, many salespeople avoid writing a proposal or write a poor quality proposal. By doing so, they damage the sales partnership. They fail to meet the buyer's expectations and put the sale at risk.

Many sales managers, who are trying to get involved in the quality movement, overlook the importance formal proposals play in the quality sales process. They may understand the need to partner with the buyer, but they do not understand how the proposal documents the partnership's activities. Instead, these managers expect propestive buyers to:

- develop internal recommendation reports for senior management
- make critical business decisions based on conversations, presentations, demonstrations, and information provided during the sales process

Important Topic

The link between quality, customer-driven sales partnerships, and formal proposals is an important topic. Important because:

- buyers are demanding cost-effective and appropriate solutions [and strategies] that meet their unique needs and help them gain competitive advantage
- buyers want to see specific, tangible proof that supports the claims made by marketing literature and salespeople
- sales proposals are direct and very tangible reflections on selling organizations

Instead, some sales professionals and their managers view proposals as minor obstacles for a salesperson to overcome in the selling process. They:

- think writing proposals is easy and that anyone within the organization can write a quality proposal
- misunderstand the "value-added" concept—a service or product has no value in itself; identifying a buyer's business problems and then effectively and efficiently implementing the service or product adds value
- lack a clear understanding of their sales staff's goals, roles, and responsibilities
- pay lip service to training—training sales professionals why it's important to write customer-driven sales proposals

These salespeople and their managers have forgotten or do not understand that a sales professional's:

- *goal* is to create an atmosphere of credibility and trust—a sales partnership
- *role* is to identify, understand and solve their buyer's business problems [or opportunities]

- *responsibility* is to accurately represent their organization's service and product capabilities and benefits in a professional manner

The Salesperson's Dilemma

To many sales professionals, quality selling and writing a quality sales proposal presents a major dilemma. Their sales managers do not understand that sales partnership activities may be difficult and time-consuming because of the need to:

* gather, organize, and interpret buyer information
* develop unique and viable business solutions
* communicate to the buyer in a professional, logical, and systematic manner

Further, many sales professionals lack the education, systems, processes, and management support for writing proposals. The time needed to develop a quality proposal usually conflicts with management's demands to identify more leads, make more calls, and close more business.

Some Reasons

Several reasons have contributed to the decline of quality in some sales organizations:

* ineffective selection and hiring processes
* selling technological advancements rather than business solutions
* the "empty suit" syndrome
* overemphasis on *superficial*, relationship selling
* short-term, profit-motive thinking

Ineffective selection and hiring processes

Many organizations fail to evaluate and profile their most successful and qualified salespeople. These organizations have no written profiles on which to base selection and hiring decisions. As a result, many of the new salespeople mirror the perceived success image of the hiring sales executive. Some of the factors that have contributed to these uninformed and incorrect hiring decisions include:

- inadequate hiring standards or no conformance to established standards
- an overemphasis on relationship skills as the most important entree to sales success
- more concern for verbal and presentation skills and personality [extrovert rather than analytical salespeople]
- little consideration for written communication skills; they only need to "talk the talk" not "walk [write] the talk"

Selling technological advancements rather than business *solutions*

New technologies affect almost all organizations. Some sales organizations do not recognize that technological advancements are only part of what they sell. They ignore the need to develop partnerships with their buyers. These organizations have lost sight of the fact that:

- technology benefits are irrelevant if they cannot be translated into business solutions
- buyers need to understand the connection between their real-world business problems or opportunities and the purported gains from technology investments

Often times technology-based organizations hire "sales technocrats" instead of sales professionals. Many of these "sales technocrats" treat selling as a knowledge and expertise contest with the buyer. These "sales technocrats" exhibit selling behaviors such as:

- overwhelming the buyer with technological jargon
- showing little empathy for the non-technical person who is afraid to ask questions
- trying to maintain a "top-dog" position with the buyer which results in a win-lose situation
- discussing only their technology rather than its application in the buyer's business

The "empty suit" syndrome

For some reason the superficial "empty suit" syndrome appears in many organizations. In these organizations, sales management spends an inordinate amount of time:

- reworking their sales forecast — their desired results
- preparing for internal presentations to advance their own careers
- planning the annual sales meeting or rally
- developing numerous excuses for their management shortcomings to avoid owning responsibility for missing the numbers
- traveling around making superficial sales calls in a feeble attempt to build buyer relationships rather than providing buyers with solutions to their business problems

Management ignores the need to establish and constantly improve partnering sales processes, systems, and education programs to obtain quality results. To the salesperson, it often appears that Rome is burning while Nero fiddles.

Overemphasis on *superficial, relationship selling*

Some salespeople think making calls and presentations is selling. They socialize with their buyers to develop relationships rather than working to develop sales partnerships. They present service or product features and expect their buyers to translate them into benefits. They do not write quality proposals that can help their buyers identify and solve complex business problems.

Writing a quality proposal requires time, effort, and management support. Many times management models the salespeople's behavior; it models the superficial and ignores the "Customer First" approach to sales partnerships.

Short-term, profit-motive thinking

An increase in global competition has led many American companies to short-term, profit-motive thinking. This creates a need for ever-increasing sales and more short-term superficial activities rather than developing sales partnerships selling. These companies ignore the need to build long-term, customer relationships. Rather they emphasize short-term results at any cost, including the cost of lost or missed sales.

Customer-Driven Sales

A sales process motivated by the customer's needs rather than those of the sales professional or the sales organization inevitably produces increased results and more satisfied customers. As an integral part of the sales partnership process, customer-driven proposals:

- focus attention on the buyer's needs
- improve buyer information gathering activities and the quality and relevancy of the information
- help establish realistic sales plans, strategies, and timeframes

What is more important, a sales partnership is a customer-driven process that wins more loyal customers.

The 80/20 Quality Rule

Identifying those activities that make a difference in sales means using the "80/20 Quality Rule." This rule states that 80% of the sales are based on 20% of the sales activities that produce 80% of the sales. These activities are critical for improvement of quality and the continuing success of the sales process.

Writing quality proposals represents a significant part of that 20%. Sales proposals are the "missing link" in many sales partnerships because they:

- focus on the buyer's needs and wants
- force the sales professional to identify the buyer's problems or opportunities

- require the sales professional to define viable business solutions and strategies
- help the buyer to make a buy decision

Processes and Tools

This book provides a variety of proven sales processes and communication tools to improve sales quality and develop sales partnerships. These process and tools will help:

- senior management develop customer-driven sales partnerships processes to enhance and improve sales
- consultants and sales professionals communicate their organization's goals for customer service, satisfaction, and quality

---

"America's workforce waits while managers decide whether to take the easy path to quick returns (and ultimate disaster) ... or use Quality Leadership to travel the road to long-term prosperity."

Peter Scholtes
The Team Handbook
(Joiner Associates, Inc., 1990)

CHAPTER 2

◆

BASIC:
A CUSTOMER-DRIVEN, QUALITY SALES SYSTEM

"Marketing...is the whole business seen from the point of view of its final result, that is, from the customer's point of view. Concern and responsibility for marketing must, therefore, permeate all areas of the enterprise."

Peter F. Drucker
The Changing World of the Executive
(Quadrangle, 1982)

Chapter Overview

In this chapter you will:

- learn about the importance of having purpose and motivation as dimensions for integrating quality into the selling
- understand the need for sales organizations to develop and implement a buyer or customer-driven, sales system
- review the rationale for developing BASIC, our quality sales system, as a means to support the concept of proposals as an important and critical element to partnership selling
- briefly examine BASIC's five, major sales processes

"As a man thinketh in his heart so is he."

James Allen

What Is the Mission?

An effective sales professional needs to develop a clear mission for selling. A sales professional's mission statement answers these questions:

- Why am I in sales?
- From my customer's or buyer's point of view, what is important in selling?

Here are excerpts from some company mission statements:

"To be of service to customers. Quite simply the best."

Boca Raton Hotel
Ted Kleisner

"To Bring Good Things To Life."

General Electric

"Quality is Job One."

Ford Motor Company

These themes provide clarity and focus for customer expectations. They become driving, motivating, and integrating forces for every task. These have purpose and motivation.

Many sales people lack purpose for why they sell; they lack a definitive personal mission statement. When asked why they sell, sales professionals' answers include:

- "I peddle to make money."
- "It's a game and I like winning."
- "I don't know, I guess just to survive."

A true mission or purpose for selling is not epitomized by the:

- old stereotype of fast-talking, huckster salesmen
- take-the-money-and-run con-artist or snake oil peddler
- "Willie Loman" types

Purpose and Motivation in Selling

When people find their purpose or identify what motivates them, they discover what energizes them to act; it provides meaning for their work. Purpose and motivation are not sales activities. Rather, by identifying and understanding his or her personal selling purpose and motivation, a sales professional establishes a grounding point that provides direction for integrating diverse, unstructured selling activities.

Having purpose and motivation means being able to answer the following question at any moment in the sales process:

- Why am I doing these things now?

A focus on purpose and motivation helps to identify and define goal-directed actions and behaviors. These actions and behaviors make a difference in how the salesperson relates to a buyer. They create a cooperative, collaborative, and consultative vision for selling with the buyer, a *sales partnership*.

More about Purpose & Motivation

Most of us have experienced times in our lives when we were working towards a purpose greater than ourselves; times when we were truly motivated. We may have worked for a political or religious cause when we worked long hours for little or no monetary reward. We were energized, motivated and committed at the end of each day. If we came up against complex and stubborn problems, we always solved them. Our attitudes were up beat, positive, enthusiastic, and responsible. We were focused on overcoming any obstacles that came our way. We had a sense of being on focus; we had purpose, motivation and meaning.

This kind of purpose or motivation comes from doing things we choose to do by creating the pathway for fulfilling our choices. Personal purpose and motivation become clear when we believe in what we are doing.

Define Self-Interests

For a salesperson to define personal purpose and motivation, it is helpful first to define self-interests in the selling situation. This means defining, in an unselfish way, personal self-interests and the buyer's self-interests. A sales professional should make two lists to clearly identify personal and the buyer's self-interests in any sales situation.

Most sales professionals will include salary and bonus on their self-interest list. Some will also list non-monetary self-interests such as:

- satisfying customers
- solving difficult business problems
- wanting social recognition
- belonging to a quality organization

Fulfilling his or her non-monetary self-interests can give the salesperson a sense of accomplishment and a feeling that he or she is doing something challenging and meaningful. Fulfilling the buyer's self-interests provides the buyer the business solutions they need or want and gives the sales professional the sale. When the buyer and seller form a partnership they work towards fulfilling their self-interests.

How to Create Purpose & Motivation for Selling

A sales professional needs to answer the following questions to find his or her purpose or motivation for selling:

- What do you believe you are doing when you are selling services or products to your buyers?
- What do you want people to say about you when it is all over?

Here are some answers:

- I am selling the highest quality product at the lowest possible price.
- She had the biggest sale in the company's history.
- I only sold what people wanted by creating mutually rewarding partnerships.
- She always created win-win relationships with her buyers.
- He was a devil to work with, but he always gave you what you wanted, when you wanted it, and how you requested it.
- We could always count on her to deliver what she promised.
- He was the only salesman that was always there ready to help or solve our problems—he seems to be our partner.
- I am successful because I always try to give the buyer what they want. I try to understand and care about them [the buyer] as people not just as a sale.

As a sales professional, define your personal purpose and motivation for selling. How do you want to be remembered by your customers or buyers?

After you have your statement written, post it where you can review it. When you feel lost in the sales process, it will:

- give meaning and purpose
- motivate you
- help you focus

Total Quality & Quality Sales

The methods of "total quality management" make the customer's concerns everyone's top priority. This means constantly improving each task and process so that the final service or product exceeds customer expectations. This type of relationship goes beyond customer satisfaction—it creates a *partnership* based on mutual concern and commitment.

Similar to total quality management, quality sales management makes the buyer's needs and wants the top priority for the sales organization. In other words, selling processes are buyer or customer-driven not driven by the needs of the sales organization or a salesperson. Quality sales management provides the sales organization with more effective (doing the right thing) and efficient (doing the thing right) selling processes.

Quality selling processes automatically lead to sales partnering. When the sales professional is driven by the needs of the buyer, he or she works towards finding business solutions to the buyer's problem or opportunity. The buyer will soon realize that the sales professional is genuinely interested in their unique business operation and trying to determine if his or her service or product offers a viable alternative. The sales partnership is mutually beneficial because the buyer solves a business problem or capitalizes on a business opportunity and the sales professional gets the deal. Typically, when a sales professional operates in a sales partnership mode, he or she provides the impetus for developing a long-term buyer-seller relationship.

A Key Point

Therefore, if a sales professional's purpose or motivation is truly buyer or customer-driven, focused on solving the buyers' business problems [or capitalizing on business opportunities], we have a dimension that:

- integrates quality in the sales process
- becomes the basis for developing a buyer-seller partnership
- satisfies the unique needs and wants of the buyer

The Need for a System

---

*"**If** a series of related tasks can be called a process, a group of related processes can then be seen as a system. Selling a product, for example, is a system that involves thousands of interrelated processes."*

Peter Scholtes
The Team Handbook
(Joiner Associates, Inc., 1990)

A sales system should offer practical and professional processes that improve the quality of sales. It should focus on improving sales by emphasizing how sales work gets accomplished (the processes) instead of simply what gets done (the results). A sales system's processes should:

- facilitate the development and nuturing of buyer-seller relationships
- assist salespeople in understanding their buyer's business problems
- base solutions and strategies on the buyer's unique needs and wants
- show how the proposed solutions and strategies will benefit the buyer's business

Above all, a sales system should constantly reinforce the often forgotten notion that without customers, there is no company.

Basis for BASIC

Over the years, people and organizations have advanced many, and often times manipulative, sales approaches. Most of these approaches focus on winning at any cost rather than on a quality, customer-driven sales system. Selling activities without an identifiable mission, structure, or system become hit or miss propositions. Some of these sales approaches claim success takes one minute; others propose eighteen easy steps to 'sales nirvana'; others want sales people to become sales athletes or use guerrilla warfare tactics.

We thought it important to offer a simple, concise, and proven professional sales system. BASIC, our quality sales system:

- provides effective and efficient processes for selling
- promotes the formation of buyer-seller relationships
- promotes the proposition that sales professionals and their sales processes must always be buyer or customer-driven
- recognizes and reinforces the buyer's need to receive at least one important and critical tangible from the sales process — a quality proposal

Over the last twenty years, we've learned a great deal about quality selling. We have:

- taught sales seminars
- sold professional consulting services and software
- made some mistakes and lost sales and did some things right and closed some big deals
- observed many successful [or lucky] and unsuccessful [or unlucky] salespeople
- built and sold a profitable company

From our experiences and observations, we developed BASIC, our buyer or customer-driven sales system. We use the acronym BASIC to symbolize what we learned. Quality selling is BASIC. Some sales professionals have made it too complex. It is less complex when the sales professional views the sale situation from the buyer's side of the desk. And, selling is much easier when the buyer and seller are partners not opponents.

Five BASIC Processes

BASIC provides a proven roadmap for quality sales. It defines five overlapping and integrated sales processes in a customer or buyer-focused sales system:

- Building Rapport and Relationships
- Auditing Operations and Organization
- Seeking and Confirming Needs and Wants
- Initiating and Presenting Solutions and Strategies
- Closing the Sale

BASIC's five processes fit into a structure which includes the "missing link" to quality selling — the proposal. The following timeline illustrates BASIC's structure for each sale:

Exhibit 2.1

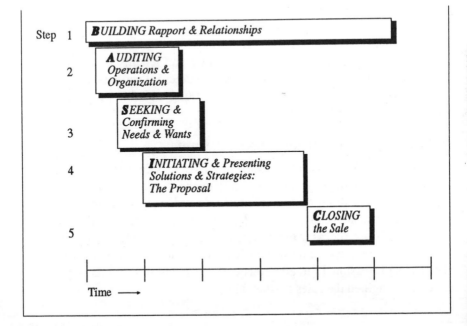

"B" Building Rapport & Relationships

It is important to establish an open and relaxed atmosphere on the initial sales call and *throughout* the selling process. We call this "Building Rapport and Relationships" with the buyer. When the sales professional is a "real" person, not presenting a front or facade, he or she is much more likely to effectively establish a positive relationship. Empathic understanding of the buyer's [person's] motives and dreams is every bit as important as developing a sales partnership that identifies and solves business problems.

"A" Auditing Operations & Organization

During BASIC's second step or process, the sales professional needs to use his or her best consultative selling skills to audit or assess the buyer's:

- business goals, functions, and strategies
- organizational structure, environment, and internal politics
- current business cycle and plans

Audit [or analysis] activities involve interaction with the buyer. This interaction facilitates the formation of a sales partnership. If the sales professional does not gather pertinent and correct information from the buyer during this process, the chances of writing a quality proposal and closing the sale are reduced or at risk.

"S" Seeking and Confirming Needs & Wants

During the third BASIC sales step or process, the sales professional must discover why the buyer would require or desire the service or product being sold. The sales professional must try to identify the pain or void for the buyer to arrive at a clear understanding of their needs and wants. The goal of this process is to agree on the problem or opportunity that will warrant the buyer and sales professional doing business together. The sales professional's interactions with the buyer during this step further strengthen the sales partnership.

"I" Initiating & Presenting Solutions & Strategies

The fourth BASIC sales step or process requires the sales professional to develop and present creative and unique business solutions or strategies. Since the buyer and seller have developed a sales partnership, these solutions and strategies will meet the buyer's expectations. During this process, the sales professional writes [and presents] a quality sales proposal. The proposal documents the seller's business solution to a mutually agreed to buyer problem or opportunity.

"C" Closing the Sale

During this last sales step or process, the sales professional asks for the business or the order. He or she handles any remaining resistance to the sale and any buyer doubts, fears, or hesitation. At this time, the sales professional needs to be patient and show empathy for the buyer's position. This may be the last step in the seller's system but it represents the first step in the buyer's internal sales system.

The sales professional must reassure the buyer that their buying decision is a good one. By following the ideas and concepts presented in this book, the buyer will hae a quality proposal that includes all the information needed to make the decision.

Some Thoughts on BASIC

By applying the principles of BASIC, consultants and sales professionals will develop solid foundations for quality selling. They will:

- see the critical links between BASIC's sales processes and writing a quality proposal
- become grounded in a customer-driven sales partnership
- view all sales activities in the context of a whole system not as isolated elements
- use BASIC and this book's proposal writing guidelines to write quality proposals and win sales

"There is no such thing as "soft sell" or "hard sell."
There is only "smart sell" and "stupid sell."

Charles Brower
President, *Batton, Barton, Durstine & Osborne*
Editor & Publisher, December 7, 1957

CHAPTER 3

◆

BUILDING RAPPORT AND RELATIONSHIPS

"If [a man] is brusque in his manner, others will not cooperate. If he is agitated in his words, they will awaken no echo in others. If he asks for something without having first established a [proper] relationship, it will not be given him."

I Ching: Book of Changes
China, c. 600 B.C.

Chapter Overview

By reading this chapter, you will:

- examine components of BASIC's first step: objectives, self-interests, trust and confidence, and selling environments
- learn about three methods to build rapport with a buyer:
  - making introductions
  - listing buyer objectives
  - explaining administrative details
- discover several concepts to consider when relating with a buyer:
  - go with what you've got
  - the "One Minute Knock-out" rule
  - good communications
  - knowledge of body language

- review the importance of good listening skills and questioning techniques
- survey the fact and feeling questioning technique and three question types:
  - opened and closed-ended
  - reflection/clarification
  - directive

 Step 1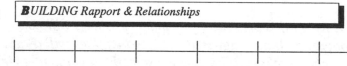

BUILDING Rapport & Relationships

Time ⟶

"B" Building Rapport and Relationships

Building rapport and relationships occurs *throughout* the sales process. It is the first process in BASIC because it is critical. For the sales professional, it represents critical behavior for establishing trust and confidence with the buyer.

Objective

The primary objective of rapport and relationship building is to reduce interpersonal conflict, tension, and the need to be defensive. If established correctly, building rapport puts the buyer at ease. Relating increases the buyer's interpersonal "zone of comfort." This ongoing sales function makes the buyer more receptive and open to the presentation of solutions and strategies.

Self-Interest: A Key Component

Most people agree, that except for unavoidable accidents, people do things for their own purposes or self-interests. Purpose and self-interest operate heavily in the selling process. People [buyers] seek to buy because they feel they have specific needs or wants. Buyers will become involved with a salesperson to:

- help themselves
- to improve their organization's productivity or profitability — make or save money

Trust and Confidence: Essential Elements

A sales professional must establish trust and confidence to help the buyer satisfy his or her needs. Building rapport and relationships becomes an essential element in establishing trust and confidence through the key counseling skills of asking questions, listening, and sharing. Effective use of these counseling skills can eliminate barriers so people [buyers] can present themselves and their organizations honestly to the sales professional.

Non-defensive Environment

Having rapport and a relationship with the buyer means:

- interacting on an equal, one-to-one basis
- feeling mutual trust and confidence
- creating an environment in which the buyer can share his or her fears, doubts, personal feelings, interests, and opinions
- accepting the buyer as an imperfect human being with a variety of feelings, motivations, and needs/wants
- creating an environment which facilitates an open exchange of information and learning

An open environment is necessary for people [buyers] to be willing to expose their problems and purposes and to accept feedback from others. Buyers appreciate this type of environment — they respond and exchange information willingly when the proper "mood" exists from the onset.

Methods of Rapport Building

There are three quality methods for establishing face-to-face rapport:

- making proper introductions
- identifying objectives of the meeting
- explaining administrative details

Rapport Method 1: Making Introductions

An effective sales professional always introduces himself or herself and his or her colleagues first. Just like introducing yourself to a new acquaintance, a sales professional always should take the lead with introductions.

A sales professional also insures that all other participants introduce themselves (or each other) to the group. Everyone should know who is involved and what their roles are for the sales call/meeting before beginning any exchange of information or a presentation.

Rapport Method 2: Listing the Buyer's Objectives

Sales professionals sometimes are so concerned with meeting their personal objectives for the sales call/meeting that they forget to consider the buyer's objectives [self-interests]. Asking the buyer to list his or her objectives keeps the sales call on target and shows empathy for the buyer's needs.

In meetings with several buyer participants, some sales professionals use the following technique to identify objectives. They:

- ask each participant to define his or her objectives for the call/meeting
- list the participants' objectives on a flip chart or blackboard to reach an understanding of the entire group's objectives

Rapport Method 3: Explaining Administrative Details

Many buyers are detail-oriented. They want to know how long the meeting will take and when they can get back to their schedule. The sales professional will take time at the beginning of the meeting to review planned duration, meals, and other administrative issues.

Covering these issues may answer many of the buyer's questions and eliminate possible problems during the call. This allows call participants to pay full attention to exchanging information and reviewing products and services.

Methods of Relating

There are a number of methods for relating with others. Some methods to increase the chances for positive interaction are:

- go with what you've got
- awareness of the "One Minute Knock-out" rule
- be a good communicator
- knowledge of body language

Relating Method 1: Go With What You've Got

People are very adept at identifying phoney and superficial behavior. Authenticity is the key to establishing trust and confidence. Identify your personality, preferences, and strengths and work with them.

Relating Method 2: The "One Minute Knock-out" Rule

" *You* never get a second chance to make a good first impression."

anonymous

A sales professional is always aware of the "One Minute Knock-out" rule. This rule states that people generally decide within the first minute of interaction whether they like you or not. During this first, critical minute, a sales professional will not say or do anything that might put-off or offend the buyer.

This rule also covers first impressions, including appearance. A sales professional dresses in a manner that mirrors the buyer's business environment, e.g., wears a conservative suit, not a casual sport suit to call on a law firm, investment company, or bank. People and buyers form quick and inflexible impressions about a person's appearance. They tend to be very critical about physical appearances and their preferences. A sales professional understands the importance of good grooming and appropriate attire. He or she avoids making a bad first impression based on appearance

Relating Method 3: Communication

Through effective communication a sales professional demonstrate flexibility, openness, and empathy. Effective communication includes listening, asking questions, and restating the buyer's position.

A sales professional will open the conversation with a topic or question in which he or she knows the buyer has interest. This allows the buyer to get comfortable (establish an interpersonal "zone of comfort" with the sales professional) and signals that the sales professional finds him or her important.

The buyer controls the power in the sales relationship not the sales professional. Therefore, the sales professional must "flex" to the buyer's needs, wants, and style. The sales professional can direct the buyer's decision to go forward with the sales relationship by being positive, friendly, and interested in the buyer's business and needs.

Relating Method 4: Body Language

Body language also plays an important role in building relationships. Some examples of how the buyer can relate to sales professional's body language include:

- a "dead fish" handshake signals weakness
- a constant, cold stare may cause uneasiness
- shifting eye focus between the buyer's eyes and chin communicates confidence and attention

- leaning forward in a chair indicates attentiveness when listening
- unflinching and sustained eye contact is the barest essential to being taken seriously

Listening

Behavior and communication experts have identified many reasons for relationship breakdowns. Demonstrating poor listening skills is one of the critical behaviors that can cause a breakdown. Listening is critical to gathering information during the selling process.

Bad Listening Habits

- trying to control the conversation to control the direction of the call [sale] or show superiority
- showing indifference to the conversation which implies the buyer has nothing important to say
- interrupting the buyer or completing the buyer's sentences shows lack of respect or patience; not trying to understand before wanting to be understood
- manipulating the conversation to cover hidden agendas or purposes to meet personal needs
- prejudging the buyer or slighting the buyer's messages because of personal prejudices
- over-generalizing personal experiences as the only correct way to do things

Good Listening Habits

- encouraging buyer involvement in the conversation
- trying to detect a central message
- not getting hung-up on mannerisms
- maintaining emotional control and suspending judgements
- avoiding or overcoming distractions
- taking notes and reflecting or restating the buyer's conversation to:
  - seek clarification
  - show understanding
  - gain agreement
  - stay on track

- demonstrating verbal and non-verbal interest in the conversation by:
    - asking the customer for more information or detail
    - nodding his or her head to indicate understanding
    - maintaining eye contact
    - using silence as a way to solicit more information
- asking open-ended questions that are relevant to the buyer's business

People and buyers like to be around and are open to a good and effective listener.

Questioning

There is no question too sensitive to ask— financial, strategic, or proprietary, as long as the sales professional has developed and nurtured the buyer's "zone of comfort." A sales professional lets the buyer know he or she needs to ask questions; to determine:

- the issues facing the buyer's organization
- whether your products or services will meet the buyer's needs

For example:

- May I ask a few questions about your organization's goals and priorities?
- What issues can you share to help me better understand your organization's strategies?

A sales professional always begins with general, easy to answer questions before moving to more complex and sensitive areas. This gives the buyer a chance to "get in gear" with the conversation and allows time to build support, trust, and credibility.

Fact and Feeling Questioning

"Fact and feeling" questioning is an effective communication technique. The salesperson presents a fact and solicits the buyer's feelings in regard to that fact.

For example, in talking face to face with the president of a telecommunication company, a sales professional might present facts and solicit feelings in the following manner:

- *Many of our customers in the telecommunication industry tell us competition is getting tighter and tougher because of deregulation (the fact). How do you feel about the deregulation situation (the solicitation for the buyer's feelings)?*
- *It's hard to get and retain good people (the fact). How does this situation affect your company (the solicitation for the buyer's feeling)?*

Open-Ended and Close-Ended Questions

Open-ended questions are designed to get the buyer to open-up and talk freely. These questions cannot be answered with a simple yes or no response. Questions that can be answered with a simple yes or no response are close-ended questions. Open-ended questions usually begin with one of the following words: what, when, where, how, or why.

Some examples:

- *What are the reasons for your company's higher employee turnover rate? (open-ended)*
- *Is lack of skills training one of the reason for high employee turnover in your company? (close-ended)*

Reflective/Clarification Questions

Reflective or clarification questions are used to:

- reflect on or clarify the buyer's thoughts or feelings about a certain situation
- clarify the buyer's answer to previous questions

Some examples:

- *By that do you mean you are frustrated with the performance of your present air delivery service?*
- *If I understand you correctly, are you saying that your present service is unreliable because ... ?*

Directive Questions

Directive questions seek specific answers to critical, qualifying information needed for you to do business together. Many times these questions become the "make or break" questions for continuing the sales call.

Some examples:

- *Does your department have the $50,000 needed to develop the video?*
- *Is your organization willing to commit two, full-time design engineers to the development team for this consulting project?*
- *What is your budget?*

CHAPTER 3 CHECKLIST

__ 1. Rapport and relationship established:

    __ proper introductions made
    __ buyer's self-interests identified
    __ trust and confidence built
    __ "zone of comfort" established

__ 2. Methods of relating:

    __ go with what you've got
    __ the "One Minute Knock-out" rule
    __ communication
    __ body language

__ 3. Effective communication skills:

    __ listening habits
    __ questioning techniques

"One of our ironclad rules is "Never do business with anybody you don't like." If you don't like somebody, there's a reason. Chances are it's because you don't trust him, and you are probably right. I don't care who it is or what guarantee you get — cash in advance or whatever. If you do business with somebody you don't like, sooner or later you'll get screwed."

Henry V. Quadracci
President, *Quad/Graphics. Inc.*
Inc. Magazine, August 1987

CHAPTER 4

◆

AUDIT•SEEK•CONFIRM

"Most people would rush ahead and implement a solution before they know what the problem is."

Q.T. Wiles
Turnaround Operations consultant
Inc. Magazine, February 1988 Step

Chapter Overview

In this chapter you will review the second BASIC step in detail and examine:

- audit objectives and length
- an audit questionnaire
- the need for an internal sponsor [partner]
- internal and external information sources

You will then learn about BASIC's third critical step and survey several major points:

- the need to reach a mutual agreement with the buyer

- when auditing stops and seeking and confirming needs and wants begins
- the requirement for good oral and written communications skills
- the importance of a Confirmation Letter

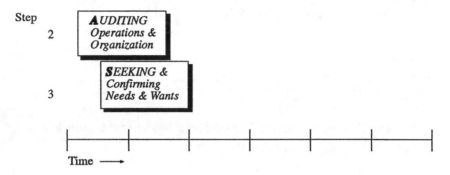

"A" Auditing Operations & Organization

During this second BASIC step, the sales professional needs to use his or her best consultative selling skills. Auditing or analyzing the buyer's current business activities and functions is a critical activity in the sales process. The salesperson can use formal or informal methods to learn about the buyer:

- What they are doing now?
- How they are doing it?
- What problems or opportunities are they facing?
- What do they plan to do in the future to attain some desired result?

The time spent working with the buyer during this step gives the sales professional an excellent opportunity to develop and nuture the sales partnership. Typically, working in a collaborative, cooperative, and consultative manner fosters the development of rapport and a relationship with the buyer. Rapport and a relationship with the buyer naturally lead to the development of a buyer-seller sales *partnership*. In this sales partnership, the buyer and seller have mutual goals—to identify a business solution to a business problem [or opportunity].

The knowledge gained in this step becomes the basis for buyer or customer-driven selling. The salesperson reduces the chances of making the sale by not gathering pertinent information during the buyer audit or analysis. Not understanding the buyer's needs and wants makes it difficult to propose a viable business solution.

Objectives

Every buyer is unique. Therefore, the preliminary objectives of the audit are to identify and understand the buyer's:

- current business operations
- level of functioning: growth cycle, steady "don't-rock-the-boat" mode, or business decline
- organizational structure and political environment
- current and potential problems and opportunities
- causes for these problems or reasons for these opportunities
- planned resolutions, projects, campaigns, etc.
- decision-making process
- key decision-makers and their interrelationships and styles

The final objective of the audit is to have a sufficient understanding of the buyer's business on which to base the next step's sales activities— Seeking and Confirming Needs and Wants.

Audit Length

There is no formula for determining how long an audit will take or how much work will be involved. Some factors that may influence the length of the audit include:

- Is the buyer a past or current customer?
- Was the sales call initiated by the buyer or a Request for Proposal (RFP)?
- Would the proposed service or product represent a major innovation or a new business venture for the buyer?

- Does the buyer have a general understanding of how the service or product can save or make money?
- Is the buyer's competition using similar services or products?
- How does the buyer view the service or product for the future success of the organization?
- Would the purchase of the service or product represent a significant cost or commitment of internal resources for the buyer's organization?
- Does the buyer have budgeted funds to buy the service or product?

The Audit [or Analysis] Process

A sales professional begins audit [or analysis] activities before the first sales call by gathering available, buyer-related information.
Therefore, on the first sales call [with a new buyer] the salesperson has three types of information:

- preliminary buyer information such as business type, annual revenues, names of senior managers and corporate officers, credit information
- knowledge about the service or product being sold
- a general idea of why the buyer might want or need the product or service

The audit process continues during the first and subsequent sales call. A sales professional uses these calls to:

- increase the scope and depth of buyer knowledge and understanding
- nuture the sales partnership

Gaining knowledge and understanding are the means to reach the next BASIC selling step: to seek and confirm valid needs and wants.

Some Thoughts

An ineffective salesperson ignores the need for the buyer audit— the need to make sales activities customer-driven. Instead, an ineffective salesperson:

- expects the buyer to justify purchase of the service or product based solely on brochures and sales presentations
- thinks building rapport and a relationship and making periodic sales calls will eventually lead to a sale
- fails to develop a buyer-seller partnership
- only tries to sell harder rather than helping the buyer to buy

When asked to audit a buyer's business, an ineffective sales professional may respond with one or more of the following statements:

I don't know how, I was never trained.
I don't have time:

- I waste too much time on one buyer.
- I can't spend that much time on one buyer, I'm required to make too many calls each month.

I don't want to:

- It's too much work, I'm in sales not consulting.
- I laid out all the benefits in my presentation. If they can't see why they need the product [service], they're fools.

These three responses demonstrate poor quality selling techniques. They deny the need to first understand the buyer's business before trying to sell solutions.

Internal Sponsor [or Champion]

Identifying and recruiting an internal sponsor [or champion] is critical to conducting an effective audit and develop a sales partnership. Typically, the sales professional identifies the sales contact as an internal sponsor. Sometimes the original contact may assign an associate to facilitate the audit.

The internal sponsor can become an invaluable guide to the audit by:

- recommending operational areas to review
- suggesting what questions to ask and information to gather
- identifying people to interview to:
  - add credibility to the audit's findings
  - establish relationships with other people in the organization who may be involved and influential in the buying decision—expand the partnership

Building rapport and a relationship with the internal sponsor is an important ingredient to a successful audit. When the internal sponsor has trust and confidence in the sales professional, he or she becomes a selling partner. The partners develop a cooperative, collaborative, and consultative relationship in which they readily share information and ideas. Together the partners identify and define the buyer's problem [or opportunity] and evaluate the viability of the seller's solution. If the seller's service or product solves the buyer's problem [or capitalizes on an opportunity], the internal sponsor *will*:

- assume ownership of the problem or opportunity
- *champion* the seller's solution within the organization

The sales partnership becomes mutually beneficial. The internal sponsor receives recognition for finding a solution to a problem or opportunity and the sales professional closes the deal.

Situational Analysis

Most sales professionals would find auditing [or analyzing] much easier if they followed a consistent approach. Using the four sides of the *Situational Analysis* model can provide structure to the audit process.

URGENT

short-term
tactics
pain

HUMAN

staffing
training
productivity
teams

systems
production
capacities

TECHNICAL

long-term
business plans
issues & trends

STRATEGIC

Audit Questionnaire

Using the four sides of the *Situational Analysis* model also makes it easy to develop an audit questionnaire. Given the uniqueness of the product or service being sold and each buyer and sales situation, most sales professionals will want to add customized questions to the following questionnaire.

Urgent:

- Does the buyer have any short-term needs or wants?
- Does the buyer have any short-term pain or opportunity?
- Is the buyer experiencing an increase or decrease in market share?
- What current business issues affect the buyer?
- What current economic, political, and legal trends affect the business and industry?
- Who are the competitors and what are they doing?
- Is the industry growing, stable, or declining?
- How profitable is the business? Does the buyer expect an increase or decrease in profitability in the current year?
- How does the buyer measure profitability and what affects profitability?

- What urgent business problems or opportunities currently face the buyer:
  - Customer service?
  - Finance and accounting?
  - Information services?
  - Marketing and sales?
  - Product or service quality?
  - Productivity?
  - Globalization?
- How important are these problems or opportunities to the buyer?
- Who in the organization has accountability and responsibility for these problems or opportunities?
- How much are these problems or opportunities affecting the company through higher costs or lost revenue?
- How did the buyer deal with similar problems or opportunities in the past and how successful were the solutions?
- Does the buyer have plans for dealing with these problems or opportunities?
- What barriers exist to resolving the problems or capitalizing on the opportunities?
- Does the buyer have budgeted funds to deal with these problems or opportunities? How much?

Technical
- How does the buyer produce its products or services?
- Is the buyer currently at an under or over-capacity position?
- What production and information systems does the buyer consider "mission-critical"?
  - How long have these systems been in place?
  - How well are these systems working?
  - Are there any capacity problems?
  - What type of information do these systems provide for managing the business?
- How has the buyer integrated these systems within the organization? Are there any problems?
- Who controls these systems?
- How do these systems affect the quality of the buyer's service or products?

Human
- What are the buyer's current staffing levels?
- Does the buyer have any employee training needs?
- Is the buyer experiencing high or low employee productivity?
- Does the buyer use the team approach to solve difficult problems, improve quality, or implement new systems?
- How is the organization structured?
- Who controls the various divisions and departments?
- Does the organization have stable leadership and management?
- Who has decision-making responsibility and at what level?
- What decision-making criteria does the organization follow?
- What issues affect the workforce today? What issues does the buyer think will affect their workforce in the future?
- How stable is the organization's workforce and how does workforce stability affect the buyer's products or service?
- Does the buyer have any immediate plans for a reorganization?
- How well do the various divisions and departments communicate with each other and what are the internal politics?
- Does the buyer's organization emphasize the use of task forces, cross-functional team problem-solving, self-directed work teams, etc?

Strategic
- What are the buyer's long-term goals and what strategic business plans does the buyer have in place? Who has responsibility for planning?
- What and how will long-term issues or trends affect the buyer's business?
- How does the planning cycle tie to the budgeting process?
- What are the buyer's future business strategies, objectives and timeframes for:
  - Expansion?
  - Reducing costs?
  - New services or products?
  - Marketing and sales?
  - Increasing profits?
  - Improving quality?
  - Differentiating themselves from the competition?
- How does the buyer prioritize their strategies and objectives?

- What future trends does the buyer think will affect its business and the industry in the next year? In the next five years?
- What financial measures does the buyer use to make major buying decisions?
- Does the buyer use cross-functional buying committees?

Internal Audit Sources

The seller has a wealth of internal information to use for the audit. These sources include:

Annual Reports

If the buyer is a publicly held corporation they will have an annual report. It may provide insight into the buyer's goals, direction, and operation.

Strategic and Business Plans

Most buyers are reluctant to provide a salesperson with a copy of their strategic or business plans. However, some buyers may provide a copy if they feel the salesperson's service or product will have a positive influence. The buyer may ask the salesperson to sign a nondisclosure agreement before releasing this type of information.

Studies and Reports

Internal studies or reports typically provide detailed information on critical problems or opportunities. For example:

- a human resource department study may identify the need to reduce costly employee turnover
- an accounting report may outline the high cost of maintaining an obsolete point-of-sale system

Project Plans, Product Development, or Market Planning Documents

Planning documents usually come after an internal study or report that identified a need or want. These documents often establish plans to change current operations, add new products, install new equipment or systems, or initiate a new marketing program.

In some instances, the salesperson's service or product may be one of the options under consideration by the team writing a planning document. If this is the case, the salesperson should try to review the internal study or report that launched the planning activities.

Interviews

Besides working with an internal champion or sponsor, the salesperson needs to gather information from other members of the buyer's organization. The types and levels of interviews will vary depending upon the complexity of the salesperson's service or product. Normally, more complex and costly services or products require more interviews.

The sales professional should try to interview the internal sponsor's manager:

- to gain an understanding of her or his perspectives
- identify higher level needs and wants
- determine his or her agenda for success

External Audit Sources

A sales professional does not overlook outside information sources. Appropriate sources depend upon the buyer's business or industry and salesperson's service or product. Properly used, these audit sources can add credibility and support financial and non-financial justifications. External sources include trade publications, books, periodicals, magazines, newspaper articles, and Dun & Bradstreet Reports.

The Audit Base

The knowledge and information gained from a buyer audit provide a basis for identifying valid, buyer or customer-driven needs and wants. Without a thorough audit the salesperson can only speculate about the buyer's situation. With the audit the salesperson can add two quality dimensions to their seeking and confirming activities, *reality* and *empathy* for the buyer's situation.

A consultative salesperson solves complex operational and organizational problems. He or she needs the foundation information gathered in the audit process to analyze the buyer's business—the analysis needed to begin seeking specific needs and wants.

"S" Seeking & Confirming Needs & Wants

"My focus is not on selling... I concentrate on providing service— I simply help clients buy what they need. I'm always in a problem-solving mode, and that puts me on the client's side of the table."

Don Ray
Financial planner and management consultant
Financial Strategies, Fall 1987

During the third step of the BASIC sales process, the sales professional identifies the buyer's needs and wants and validates them with the buyer. The sales professional must find valid business problems or opportunities and the buyer must agree with the these findings. In the context of a sales partnership, the buyer and the seller arrive at a mutual understanding—a reason for doing business together.

When "A" Stops and "S" Begins

This third BASIC step may overlap the second step. There is no magic time to stop auditing and begin seeking and confirming needs and wants. The buyer's needs and wants may become readily apparent during the audit or they may require extensive analysis that can only be done after the audit is complete.

Communications Strategies Key

Effective communications strategies provide the key to successfully seeking and confirming valid buyer business problems or opportunities. A sales professional knows successful buyer or customer-driven selling is dependent on communicating with the buyer. Communications strategies that include:

* giving information
* receiving and properly processing information
* providing accurate and appropriate feedback

In a sales partnership the buyer and seller create a dialog where one person exchanges information or thoughts with another to achieve mutual understanding. This requires active questioning and listening skills. In addition, the sales professional must interpret the information received and communicate thoughts and ideas back to the buyer.

Many salespeople find it difficult to say or write what they mean. They assume that the buyer understands even if their speech or writing is unclear. This assumption represents one of the most difficult barriers to effective and successful communication. Rather than gaining agreement on the buyer's business problems or opportunities an ineffective sales-person often creates mutual misunderstanding.

The Confirmation Letter

Some sales professionals follow-up every call with a written message. The end of BASIC's Step 3 presents an ideal opportunity to use a Confirmation Letter. Besides demonstrating empathy, a Confirmation Letter shows responsiveness and provides the buyer with a tangible or deliverable from their participation in the sales process. It documents the sales partnership's understanding and agreement to a point in the sales cycle.

A sales professional who concisely communicates an understanding of the buyer's needs and wants has a clear direction for formulating a solution or strategy. Clear communication reflects an effective buyer-seller partnership and a probable fit that will make it easier for the buyer to buy.

The Confirmation Letter should:

- show an understanding of the buyer's unique business objectives and problems
- ensure agreement—the buyer's expectations should match the seller's perceptions
- briefly review and confirm the agreed upon needs and wants
- identify the next step or activity in the sales process

Confirmation Letter Structure

The following outline briefly identifies a Confirmation Letter structure:

Opening:

Start with a positive statement focusing on the buyer's achievements and challenges. This opening must grab the reader's attention and encourage further reading.

Purpose:

Identify the purpose for writing the letter. This section should contain a confirmation of the buyer's needs and wants. It should identify the global issue and problem or opportunity and discuss why it is important. This section should explain how the problem or opportunity relates to increased revenues or lower costs.

Potential Solution:

Include one or two sentences that briefly discuss your potential solution or approach. This section should also include a brief discussion of similar applications, your or your company's reputation, and/or benefits that the buyer will realize. It should give the buyer assurance of your or your company's capabilities.

Action Plan:

Identify the action you or your company will take as a result of the audit and this letter. If necessary, include any action the buyer may need to take.

Closing:

Include one or two sentences targeted at achieving the buyer's goals and describe how you intend to create a partnership to achieve these goals.

P.S.:

Include any final comments that link you or your company to a promise or premium. The P.S. should contain one added piece of useful information to make the buyer feel they have already received value from your company. Note: The "P.S." can be typed or hand-written.

Exhibit 4.1

Towrite Trailers
2750 South Oakland Avenue
Canton, Texas 75123

June 4, 1993

Mr. J. Roger Mayer, President
Sea Sled Boats
4485 West Corporate Park
Memphis, Tennessee 41307

Dear Roger:

Achieving sales goals in a competitive economy cannot be left to chance or old methods. Sea Sled Boats and Towrite Trailers might be able to identify specific ways to make a value difference for boat buyers.

The day we spent together at your plant was most informative and enlightening. As you know, I am a boating enthusiast and really enjoyed the cruise we took in your company's new 21' Coastal Cruiser model. I was very impressed with the exceptional handling and speed you have been able to reach with such a small engine. I think Towrite Trailers can help you improve sales performance with its quality trailers.

The purpose of this letter is to confirm my understanding of Sea Sled's plans to begin marketing their boats with custom trailers in 1993. You also expressed your company's goal to make 10-15% on custom trailers packaged and sold with its boats. Because of Sea Sled's innovative hull design, most generic trailers will not properly accommodate your boats. We identified that Sea Sled's management and its dealers feel they could increase sales by 25-35% if your boats were available with custom trailers. Unfortunately, Sea Sled's experience with a local custom trailer manufacturer was a disaster—high prices and poor quality.

I have reviewed your concerns with our production and engineering staffs. They have begun working on preliminary specifications and costs to determine if Towrite can meet your design and price needs. I want you to know that we pledge to work harder than any of our competitors to develop the highest quality product. It is Towrite Trailer's commitment to deliver complete, customer satisfaction through market-driven quality. As you stated, we have the reputation for being the best in the industry.

After our staff develops the preliminary specifications and prices for Sea Sled Boats, I would suggest we meet at our facilities. This would give you an opportunity to tour our plant and talk with some of our key people. I will contact you early next week to give you the preliminary information and to set our next meeting.

I think a partnering arrangement could be a win-win for both our organizations and customers.

Sincerely,

William F. Krause
William F. Krause
National Sales Manager

P.S. I have enclosed an article from the Texas Mfg's Journal that discusses our quality manufacturing process and customer service. I hope you find it informative and reassuring — we Walk the Talk on quality.

Final Thoughts

Many salespeople overlook a critical sales step— confirming the buyer's needs and wants. The sales professional must constantly focus on one objective—insure agreement of the needs and wants at the highest possible level in the buyer's organization. Ironically, most sales professionals are well trained to identify a buyer's needs and wants, but many forget to confirm their understanding of them with the buyer. Perhaps some sales professionals become so focused on their product or service that they assume the buyer can clearly see the benefits. For others, confirming a buyer's unique needs and wants requires more work than they care to do. However, a written confirmation of the buyer's needs and wants at this point in the sale process will:

- ensure that buyer's expectations match seller's perceptions
- keep the sales process and partnership moving forward
- give the sales professional a reason and opportunity to follow-up with the buyer
- demonstrate the sales professional's quality selling dimensions:
    - *empathy* because of his or her desire first *to understand the buyer's business and needs and wants*
    - *responsiveness* throught his or her willingness to work closely with the buyer *to identify and define business problems or opportunities*
    - *reliability* by *providing solutions or strategies for solving business problems or capitalizing on business opportunities*

CHAPTER 4 CHECKLIST

___ 1. Internal sponsor recruited.

___ 2. Custom audit questionnaire developed.

___ 3. Buyer audit completed:

    ___ external and internal information gathered

    ___ interviews completed

    ___ essential audit questions answered

___ 4. Confirmation Letter written.

CHAPTER 5

◆

INITIATING AND PRESENTING SOLUTIONS AND STRATEGIES

Step 4

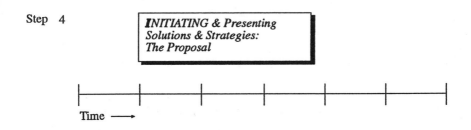

*INITIATING & Presenting
Solutions & Strategies:
The Proposal*

Time ⟶

Chapter Overview

By reading this chapter you will understand the importance of doing your homework before initiating and presenting solutions and strategies — insure your proposed service or product:

- meets the buyer's needs and wants
- offers a financially justifiable solution
- fits the buyer's timeframe

Next, you will be presented with variables that can influence timing. The:

- complexity and cost of your proposed solution
- buyer's budgetary cycle
- buyer's business plans and timeframes

You will then examine an "Expectation/Perceptions Gap" concept and learn how to reduce it.

Finally, you will learn about when to use the pre-proposal letter and review an example letter.

Do Your Homework First

After you complete your audit and confirm the buyer's needs and wants, it is time to do some homework. Do it before you initiate and present your solutions or strategies to the buyer. First convince yourself that your proposed service or product satisfies the buyer's needs and wants before trying to convince your buyer. You must have solid answers to the following questions:

- Does my solution/strategy meet the buyer's needs or wants?

  Example: *Your company sells the best inventory control system for mainframe computers. Based on your buyer's long-range MIS Plan, you know the company will move to totally decentralized operations using personal computers and local area networks over the next two years. Unless your company has concrete plans or is currently developing this type of system, you probably will waste your time and your organization's money trying to sell the buyer.*

- Can I offer a financially justifiable solution or strategy to the buyer?

  Example: *Your buyer is enamoured with the potential use of computer-based training (CBT) to instruct their seventy-five (75) senior systems engineers on the use of their very complex, telecommunications system. After reviewing the buyer's training requirements and current training costs, you estimate your proposed CBT course development fees. Through your calculations, you realize the buyer would need at least 300 students to justify CBT courseware development. You need to share your findings with the buyer before going any further.*

- Does my estimated project or implementation schedule fit the buyer's timeframe?

  Example: *Your buyer wants to complete their new manufacturing facility in six months. You estimate the project would require two months to design and obtain the necessary permits. Actual construction would require an estimated four months. Your entire crew is in the middle of a six-month project. You should review your situation with the buyer before introducing your solutions.*

If you feel unsure of your answers to these three questions, review your findings with your internal sponsor. Remember, quality selling is buyer or customer-driven. If you have developed a sales partnership, you should have little difficulty getting help from the buyer. Do not try to sell the buyer an unworkable or partial solution.

One of two things can happen when you review your findings with your internal sponsor:

- You will get confirmation and agreement that you do not need to write a proposal.
- Your internal sponsor will support your answers but will have some alternative views or provide you with other reasons to move forward.

  Example: *In a previous example, the buyer needed at least 300 students to justify the proposed CBT development project, but only had 75 internal students. If your internal sponsor reveals that the company plans to market their system nationwide and wants CBT to differentiate its product, you have an added dimension for justifying the cost.*

Homework Help

You may want and need help with your homework. Unless you can unilaterally commit resources, establish fees/prices, and set schedules and deadlines, you will need to work within your organization to complete your homework. A later chapter introduces the Proposal Team and discusses this concept in more detail.

Proposal Timing Variables

It is important to confirm the need for a proposal after you and the buyer agree that you or your organization can provide solutions or strategies. You will use a Pre-proposal Letter for this purpose.

Some variables that can influence your timing include:

The complexity and cost of your solution

The buyer measures complexity and cost, not you. Usually the more complex and costly your solution, the longer it will take to reach the pre-proposal point. You may have to make several presentations and demonstrations to satisfy the buyer's concerns regarding the applicability of your service or product. If your service or product is highly technical, you may need to schedule meetings between the buyer's and your organization's support staff to resolve technical issues.

You can only overcome a buyer's cost concerns by identifying the areas in which your solutions or strategies offer financial opportunities. Remember, your proposal must quantify expense reductions or revenue-making opportunities. However, before you write the proposal, the buyer may ask you to provide financial examples based on information gathered during your audit or examples from past or existing customers.

The buyer's budgetary cycle

If the buyer did not budget for your service or product during the current fiscal year, you may want to delay writing a proposal. However, do not delay confirming the buyer's agreement on your solutions or strategies. You also can use the Pre-proposal Letter to confirm the future timing of your proposal.

Waiting to write a proposal for delivery at the start of your buyer's budgeting cycle helps insure that your proposal will receive consideration for inclusion in next year's budget and reflects your most current fees and prices.

The buyer's project plans and timeframes

Remember, your solution must fit into the buyer's agenda. The purchase of your service or product and the timing of your Pre-proposal Letter may have to coordinate with such things as the:

- expiration of an existing contract
- implementation of a new system
- completion of a reorganization
- purchase of new equipment
- hiring of a new employee or group of employees
- acquisition of another company
- development of a new product or marketing campaign

The Expectations/Perceptions Gap

You can improve the quality of your proposal by reducing the gap between the buyer's expectations and your perceptions. Your buyer has expectations for your solutions, strategies and proposal; they probably differ from your perceptions. Developing a sales partnership helps reduce the Expectations/Perceptions Gap. The partnership fosters the free exchange of information between the buyer and seller. Further, our internal champion or sponsor should have a good idea about what it will take to sell your service or product into the organization. Before you begin to formulate solutions or strategies, ask your buyer the following questions:

- What do you expect from the proposed service or product?
- What ultimately will it take to sell the proposed service or product to your organization?

Often, the buyer's responses will alert you to:

- some item(s) that you might have overlooked or did not perceive as important
- the need for your proposal to emphasize a particular benefit or area, e.g., cost savings, your implementation strategies, schedules, etc.

The Pre-Proposal Letter

The Pre-proposal Letter represents the culmination of all previous sales activities with the buyer. It confirms your agreement with the buyer to write a proposal. The Pre-proposal Letter should contain one or two paragraphs on each of the following topics:

- background information on the buyer's business and the mutually identified needs and wants
- a brief description of your proposed service or product [solution or strategy]
- preliminary financial and non-financial justifications
- a description of the proposed project or product implementation timeframes

Optionally, the Pre-proposal Letter could delay the proposal until some future date.

To insure that your Pre-proposal Letter includes all critical information and closes the "Expectation/Perception Gap," you should write the Pre-proposal Letter and develop your proposal outline at the same time. Chapter 9 discusses the proposal outline in detail.

The following pages contain an example of a Pre-proposal Letter.

"I am a strong believer in transacting official business by the written word."

Winston Churchill

Exhibit 5.1

BankPower Software, Inc.
5950 North Dallas Parkway
Dallas, Texas 75287-1035

May 4, 1993

Mr. Charles Jones
Executive Vice President
First National Bank
123 Commerce Street
Dallas, Texas 75201

Dear Charles:

Thank you again for taking time from your busy schedule to help me gather daily processing, transaction, and customer servicing information on your commercial checking accounts. As we discovered, your Bank currently provides various types of cash management services manually to their 1,450 commercial checking customers. These services include:

- *account reconciliation processing*
- *balance requests*
- *intra-account transfers*
- *facsimile balance and paid transaction reporting*
- *wire transfer requests*
- *ACH transaction processing*
- *coin and currency requests*

On the basis of our information gathering activities and analyses, we discovered your Bank's fee income from these services barely covers your costs. We concluded your Bank experiences high costs because your cash management services are labor-intensive. As I presented, our turnkey BankPower Cash Management System offers an opportunity to reduce your Bank's cash management services' processing costs by 50-90%. Further, installing BankPower offers the ability to increase current charges because it will enhance both the quality and functionality of your cash management services.

All 35 of our customer banks have also realized several important benefits from installing BankPower:

- *the ability to attract and retain profitable, new commercial business*
- *an improved image within their trade areas — progressive and innovative*
- *a new defensive weapon to compete effectively with the larger regional banks' attempt to take away existing customers*

As you realized from your conversations with several of our customers, BankPower is an easy system to install and operate:

- *average installation takes less than two months*
- *typically requires less than ten hours per week of operator tasks*

My preliminary analyses indicate your Bank's five-year return on investment will range from 25-40% for your $30,000.00 BankPower System investment. Further, your Bank should reach a break-even point after it signs up 40-50 commercial customers. I base this break-even point upon our previous experiences with other banks your size.

Charles, as we agreed, developing a formal proposal is the next step. You want to present the proposal at the Board of Directors Meeting scheduled for May 24, 1993. I will have an outline of the proposal available for your review early next week. We can use this outline to review the proposal's content and structure. I will deliver the final proposal to you by May 21. Please let me know how many copies you will need for your Board Meeting.

Charles, thank you again for your cooperation and support. I look forward to working with you and your staff in the future.

Sincerely,

Scott L. Meyer
Account Executive

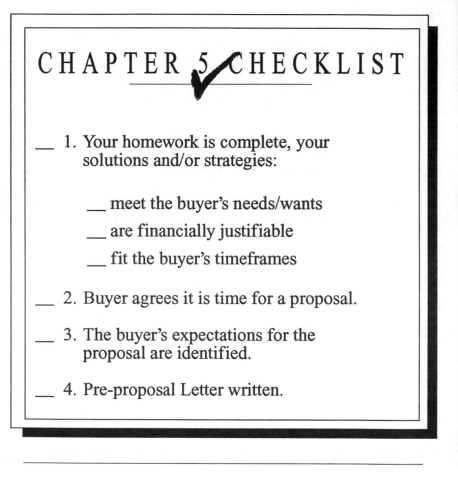

CHAPTER 5 CHECKLIST

___ 1. Your homework is complete, your solutions and/or strategies:

    ___ meet the buyer's needs/wants

    ___ are financially justifiable

    ___ fit the buyer's timeframes

___ 2. Buyer agrees it is time for a proposal.

___ 3. The buyer's expectations for the proposal are identified.

___ 4. Pre-proposal Letter written.

"*It is not the quantity, but the pertinence [of your words] that does the business.*"

Seneca, 4 B.C.-A.D. 65
Roman writer and rhetorician
Epistles to Lucilius

CHAPTER 6

◆

THE SEVEN DEADLY MISTAKES

"Experience is the name everyone gives to their mistakes."

Oscar Wilde, 1854-1900
Irish poet, playwright and novelist
Lady Windermere's Fan

Chapter Overview

In this chapter, you will learn about "The Seven Deadly Mistakes" of proposal writing. They represent the most recurrent errors, omissions, and abuses we have experienced in other organizations, identified through our research, and made in some of our past proposals.

The Seven Deadly Mistakes are:

1. Not writing a proposal
2. Not understanding the buyer's business
3. Missing the buyer's or your proposal deadline
4. Producing a proposal with little "drive-up" appeal
5. Not saying anything that makes a difference
6. Using a boilerplate approach
7. No one owning the responsibility or having the authority to create quality proposals

#1: Not Writing a Proposal

We listed this mistake as number one, simply because it is. Most consultants and salespersons dread writing proposals. They think rapport and relationships, their reputation, or the reputation of their service or product is all that is needed to get a signed contract. They often substitute a capability or product brochure and a cover letter or price quote for a formal proposal. This is a major mistake and it invariably becomes an expensive shortcut.

Buyers think they have unique situations and needs — they do. A written proposal acknowledges understanding and agreement that each buyer is unique. Even if the service or product has little latitude for providing more than a generic solution, a proposal verifies recognition of the buyer's unique business environment.

Buyers want to feel important. Buyers are people and like to feel they are important. To the consultant or salesperson looking for a signed contract, each buyer is important. Writing a proposal reinforces the buyer's sense of importance to the salesperson and his or her organization.

Buyers want and need more than talk. A proposal helps avoid the "tell them/sell them" syndrome. Not writing a proposal places heavy reliance on the salesperson's ability to verbally sell a service or product. The buyer may perceive generalized capability and cost saving/revenue enhancing statements as little more than a standard sales pitch. A proposal forces the salesperson to document financial and non-financial claims.

Not writing a proposal also means the salesperson's internal sponsor must rely on his or her memory to sell internally — sell the proposed solution or strategy based solely on what he or she remembered from sales calls and presentations. Why do so many salespeople want to take this risk?

Substituting a slick presentation for a proposal often reinforces a buyer's fear of salespeople. Unfortunately, selling is often seen as manipulative

— it takes the 'sales warrior' approach of "let's take what we have and talk someone into buying it." Conversely, helping the buyer to buy takes a consultative approach of "let's find out about the buyer's business so our service or product can help them do a better job — let's see if we can match or exceed their needs with what we offer."

#2: Not Understanding the Buyer's Business

A quality proposal explains how a service or product affects the buyer's business. Therefore, a proposal must reflect a thorough understanding of the buyer's unique goals, needs, and operations. Normally, a buyer will quit reading a proposal as soon as he or she realizes the proposal writer does not understand their business.

#3: Missing the Buyer's or Your Proposal Deadline

If a salesperson wants to send the wrong signal to the buyer, he or she only needs to miss the proposal's completion deadline — the deadline established by the buyer or the one promised by the salesperson. This implies the proposing organization probably will miss critical project or product implementation deadlines. This action demonstrates an inability to perform as promised. It communicates in behavior, not words, the organization's dependability and reliability.

This mistake may cost the proposing organization the contract if there is little differentiation between their's and the competition's services and products. Breaking a commitment can also damage the salesperson's rapport and relationship with the buyer. This type of damage is difficult to repair.

#4: Producing a Proposal with Little "Drive-Up" Appeal

Have you ever bought or sold a house? Then you know that initial impressions make a difference — does the house have good "drive-up appeal"? A buyer may establish inaccurate perceptions based solely upon a proposal's initial impression. Although some people think this idea is superficial, the proposal's physical appearance can, and often does, make a big difference.

#5: Not Saying Anything That Makes a Difference

We also call this mistake the "so what" syndrome. It can be observed in buyers who read proposals that lack cost-justification; after reading the proposal, the buyer says "so what." This response usually means no contract.

A buyer has two primary reasons to sign a contract, the proposed service or product must either reduce expenses or increase revenues — save money or make money. A proposal that fails to address the buyer's financial benefits has little chance of acceptance.

#6: Using a Boilerplate [Cookie-Cutter] Approach

Using a boilerplate approach sends a strong message to a buyer: the proposing organization thinks all customers [buyers] have the same and unchanging goals, needs, and operations. A boilerplate proposal also implies:

* lack of consultative training and the skills required to understand the buyer's business
* stagnant, or no unique services or products
* the buyer is unimportant to the salesperson — not worth the effort to write a quality proposal
* understaffing and the inability to serve the buyer's needs

Boilerplate proposals also represent a technological phenomenon of the 80s. Word processing systems provide the facilities to easily cut and paste sections from past proposals. Over time, some organization's proposals become patchworks of unfocused, illogical, and non-empathic statements.

#7: No One Owning Responsibility or Having the Authority to Create Quality Proposals

This last mistake reflects management shortcomings within an organization. It supports Dr. W. Edwards Deming's and Dr. Joseph M. Juran's

85/15 Rule: 85% of the problems are the result of management controlled systems, the remaining 15% are under the employees control.

Some causes for making this mistake include:

Lack of sales leadership. Having no one with a leadership passion, spearheading the effort, and driving the organization to deliver outstanding, quality proposals.

Indifference to quality. Failing to understand that poor quality proposals, poor quality in content and appearance, are direct reflections on the organization.

Over-emphasizing rapport and relationship building. Expecting salespeople to sell by making repetitive and purposeless sales calls solely to build rapport and relationships is inefficient. To promote socializing as the organization's primary selling technique is short-sighted. Understanding the need to formally document the buyer's reasons for doing business with the selling organization is a critical part of the sales process.

Not establishing quality proposal standards. Writing proposals without first setting quality standards for the organization's proposals is ignoring the need for a quality process.

Not establishing proposal writing processes and teams. Delegating, by default, proposal writing to anyone without regard for that person's training, ability, or authority. Failing to institute proposal writing processes and procedures to support the sales staff. Not including, in the writing process, other areas of the organization that will be affected by the proposal.

Not providing systems. Ignoring the need to provide internal and/or external proposal writing resources for the sales staff, e.g., word processing computers, printers, binding machines, etc.

Not constantly improving proposals. Failing to critique each proposal success and failure as a means of improving future proposals. Ignoring the attributes of the competition's winning proposals to improve the organization's future proposals. Discounting the need to obtain buyer feedback on the specific reasons for not getting a contract.

Not training the staff. Assuming every salesperson hired has consultative selling skills and the ability to write quality proposals. Ignoring the need to educate all members of the organization involved in writing proposals.

Final Thoughts

These are some of the mistakes we have seen in various organizations or have made ourselves. We do not think this is an all encompassing list. The important concepts to keep in mind are:

- people learn by making mistakes
- an empowering leader supports mistakes because it encourages innovation and risk-taking
- an organization needs to be proactive in avoiding the deadly mistakes by confronting internal problems and recognizing how they contribute to poor sales

---

"Aim of Leadership. The aim of leadership should be to improve the performance of man and machine, to improve quality, to increase output, and simultaneously to bring pride of workmanship to people."

W. Edwards Deming
Out of the Crisis, 10th Printing
Massachusetts Institute of Technology, August 1990

CHAPTER 7

◆

WHY AND HOW A QUALITY PROPOSAL MAKES THE DIFFERENCE

"If you are going to put your name on all your products, you should never produce a bad product. If you make a mistake, you'll hurt the whole company."

Bruno Bic
Vice President of Sales and Marketing, Bic Pen Co.
Alsop and Abrams, *The Wall Street Journal on Marketing* (Dow Jones-Irwin, 1986)

Chapter Overview

In this chapter, you will:

- learn why and how a quality proposal makes a difference in selling
- examine basic quality proposal concepts you must use to develop winning proposals
- be introduced to the five dimensions of a quality proposal:
  - **Reliability**
  - **Assurance**
  - **Tangibles**
  - **Empathy**
  - **Responsiveness**

- examine the "walk the talk" concept and learn why your proposal must clearly show the buyer how they can save or make money
- understand why your proposal must:
  - assure your buyer of your organization's abilities and capabilities
  - include Assurance Tangibles — project or implementation intangibles converted to tangibles
- understand the importance of responsiveness which you can easily demonstrate by producing the proposal in a timely manner, and showing a willingness to provide solutions
- learn why and how a quality proposal:
  - is a tangible itself
  - provides a communications vehicle into the buyer's organization
  - helps your internal sponsor sell your solutions and strategies

The chapter ends with the Quality Proposal RATER; a proposal rating questionnaire and chart that you can use to:

- discover the weaknesses in your current proposals
- measure the quality and effectiveness of your future proposals
- analyze your competitor's proposals

Quality Selling and Proposal Dimensions

In their book, *Delivering Quality Service*, Valerie A. Zeithaml, A. Parasuraman, and Leonard L. Berry, relate their years of quality customer service research. Their book identifies five dimensions essential for delivering quality customer service: reliability, assurance, tangibles, empathy, and responsiveness. In other words, for customer service to reach quality levels, it must embody these five quality dimensions. However, the authors identified *realibility* as the most critical dimension. Above all, service providers must be reliable and do what they say they are going to do.

If reliability is the most critical quality customer service dimension, then it is also the most critical quality dimension for selling and sales proposals. Sales professionals must do what they say they will do and sales proposals must reflect the selling organization's ability to do what it says it will do. In other words:

- sales professionals must keep the promises and commitments made to the buyer during and after the sales cycle
- the seller's services or products must provide specific buyer financial and non-financial benefits based on the buyer's business operation (needs and wants)
- the sales proposal must reflect the seller's ability to realistically implement, install, or produce the services or products to meet the buyer's needs and wants

Quality Proposal Dimensions

If *selling is customer service during the sale*, then it is possible to evaluate sales activities using the five quality customer service dimensions. And, if a proposal is a tangible or deliverable from the sales process, then it is also possible to evaluate sales proposal quality using the five dimensions. Therefore, adapting the five quality customer service dimensions to evaluate proposal quality, provides the following *quality proposal dimensions*:

Reliability:	reflects your [the seller's] ability to identify creative, dependable, and realistic solutions and strategies, and match them to the buyer's needs and wants
Assurance:	builds the buyer's trust and confidence in your [the seller's] ability to deliver, implement, produce, service, and/or provide the benefits
Tangibles:	enhances and supports the communication of your [the seller's] message and invites readership by its overall appearance, content, and organization
Empathy:	confirms your [the seller's] thorough understanding of the buyer's business and their specific needs and wants
Responsiveness:	developed in a timely manner and demonstrates a willingness to provide solutions for the buyer's needs and wants and to help measure results

These five quality proposal dimensions provide valuable insight into the attributes of a winning sales proposal. The *Quality Proposal RATER*, a questionnaire found at the end of this chapter, uses these five dimensions to quantify proposal quality and thereby identify a proposal's strengths and weaknesses.

Walk the Talk

Your buyer has only two primary reasons to justify contracting for your services and products. Your service or product must:

- *Save Money* by reducing an expense or category of expenses
- *Make Money* by adding a new revenue source or improving the incremental profits of an existing revenue source

If you do not agree with these two primary reasons, think about your last several contracts and why you won out over your competition. Further, review the purchases your organization has made. Did these reasons apply?

Some people suggest organizations also make purchase decisions to improve productivity or quality—add value. Both of these reasons do translate into cost reductions or revenue improvements:

- improved productivity means the same resources can produce at a higher level (or fewer resources can produce at the same level)
- improved quality results in less rework and scrap, better services and products, higher customer retention, more business [revenue], and higher profits

Walk the Talk Examples

A quality proposal must "walk the talk" by supporting the financial claims made by the sales professional or in the seller's marketing materials. A winning proposal needs to prove that the proposed service or product will deliver the financial benefits promised. "Walk the talk" examples must satisfy two of the five quality dimensions:

Reliability: reflects your ability to identify creative, dependable, and realistic solutions and strategies, and match them to the buyer's needs and wants

Empathy: confirms your thorough understanding of the buyer's business and their specific needs and wants

Further, you will need to prove your justifications using the buyer's current operation as a basis. You must develop specific quantifiable justifications or benefits based on the buyer's business operation—number of employees, annual production volumes, number of machines, etc. Vague financial benefits have little value for a buyer who has to commit the organization's financial resources. Most buyers would not make a buying decision if a proposal contained a vague statement such as "the product will reduce maintenance costs by 10%-25%." Buyers want to see financial benefit estimates based on their unique operation. They want to know how much money the seller's proposed service or product will make or save for their organization.

Calculating specific financial benefits is not easy work. It involves gathering and interpreting buyer information and using this information to calculate meaningful financial benefits for the buyer, e.g., years to payback, return on investment, and increased earnings per share. However, if the sales professional has developed a partnership with the buyer, developing financial benefits will be easier. The buyer will help with the information gathering and interpretation. For example:

SPECIFIC	VAGUE
The proposed computer-based training course will reduce your current operator training costs by $625,000 over the next four years.	*The proposed computer-based training course will reduce operator training costs after it is installed.*
Once implemented, our new integrated system will improve the efficiency of your inventory, billing, and accounts receivable processes by 40%. This will allow you to reduce your clerical support functions by four positions for an annual cost savings of $100,000.	*Once implemented, our new integrated system will improve the efficiency of your inventory, billing, and accounts receivable processes.*
The cash management system will reduce by 90% the further erosion of your commercial customer base. By offering the new service, your bank will add an estimated $220,000 of fee-based revenue over the next three years.	*The cash management system will reduce the erosion of your customer base and increase the bank's fee-based revenue.*

Walk the Talk Exceptions

Rarely, will you uncover a buyer who does not need or want financial justification to do business with you or your organization. There are three exceptions to this rule. Typically, your service or product may need to represent two or more of these exceptions:

Reputation: You have an unquestionable reputation as being the best in your field, e.g., Porsche, Albert Einstein.

Monopoly: Your product lacks competition, e.g., electricity from an electric utility company.

Innovation: You offer a creative and ingenious service or product. Your engagement or the product implementation will clearly differentiate your buyer from its competitors, for example, Jonas Salk as a medical research consultant or the first commercial airliner with jet engines.

If you think your service or product clearly represents two or more of these exceptions, stop reading right now. Still, put this book in a convenient place because your competitive advantage may be short-lived. Success today does not guarantee success tomorrow. Often success breeds overconfidence and complacency. There are many examples of companies that failed miserably after introducing one or two highly successful products or services.

Abilities and Capabilities

After your proposal meets one or both of the primary reasons a buyer must have to sign a contract, it must then document your abilities and capabilities. In other words, the proposal must meet another of the five dimensions of quality:

Assurance: builds the buyer's trust and confidence in your ability to deliver, implement, produce, service, and/or provide the benefits

By using good consulting [or solution selling] skills, you can provide your buyer with the assurance they need for signing a contract. Your project management techniques, product implementation strategies, or business practices must support your ability to execute the contract.

Assurance Examples—Turning Intangibles to Tangibles

To develop the assurance dimension in your proposal, you need to thoroughly understand the buyer's needs, wants, and business operations. You then must take the intangible aspects of your service or product and make them tangible for the buyer in the context of the buyer's unique situation. Buyers more readily make buying decisions if they believe the intangibles associated with the seller's proposal will make a difference in the overall purchase and in achieving their unique business goals. Therefore, you also must describe your service or product in terms of their non-financial or intangible impacts on the buyer's business. The proposal must turn intangibles into tangibles and thereby give the buyer assurance that the seller's proposed solution or strategy will work.

Turning most seller intangibles into unique tangibles for the buyer usually require an in-depth understanding of the buyer's business operations. This supports the need for the sales professional to develop a collaborative, consultative, and cooperative sales partnership with the buyer.

Some buyer-unique assurance examples include:

Our Plus 2000 General Ledger System will automatically interface with your existing ABC Accounts Payable and Inventory Control systems using our standard data conversion module.

My Team Building seminar will become an integral component of your two-year "Total Quality Improvement" program by providing a clear understanding of:

• how teams are formed and incented

- *how team members working together can become more effective problem-solvers*
- *how to establish team member roles and responsibilities to improve the level and quality of service in your catalog order processing operation*

Our PowerBank Cash Management System will display and support your bank's leadership role and goal to offer the most innovative commercial services in the metropolitan area.

To further satisfy the assurance dimension, your proposal must imply your [the selling organization's] ability to perform on the contract. In other words, can you [or your organization]:

- produce the product or provide the service
- implement the product or service
- deliver the benefits described in the proposal
- provide ongoing customer service

Therefore, the proposal must describe how the seller does business by including:

- production capabilities and facilities
- project or implementation plans, techniques, or methodologies
- business practices
- customer service resources
- research and development resources

The proposal must minimize the buyer's perceived risk for doing business with the seller by turning the intangible aspects of the seller's product or service into tangibles. Developing a sales partnership helps the sales professional understand how to convey confidence and trust in the proposal. In a sales partnership the sales professional gains a clear understanding of the buyer's concerns for doing business with the seller. The sales professional can then develop assurance tangibles to address the buyer's concerns—reduce the buyer's perceived risk.

Some assurance examples that turn intangibles about the seller into tangibles include:

We follow a three-step approach when installing the X2001 Office Communication System:

1. Service and Site Planning
2. Installation and Testing
3. Client Training and Conversion

We can support your new Point of Sale System conversion schedule by coordinating the installation of our PDN-3 Terminals at your 235 retail locations over the next eighteen months:

Satisfying the assurance dimension reduces the perceived risk for the buyer. Effectively satisfying the assurance dimension can also partially satisfy another quality dimension:

Tangibles: enhances and supports the communication of your message and invites readership by its overall appearance, content, and organization

Assurance Tangibles represent the intangible elements of seller's proposed project or product implementation into tangibles. This conversion may be more important for consulting projects that provide a service than for product implementations. In either case, your proposal needs to include some or all of the following Assurance Tangibles:

- *Deadlines*: estimated project or implementation completion dates for various tasks or activities

- *Deliverables*: documents, events, or products that record completion of tasks and activities

- *Signoffs*: opportunities throughout the project or implementation for your buyer to approve your deliverables

- *Staffing*: your estimated staffing levels for the project or implementation

- *Facilities*: descriptions of your production and support facilities, equipment, and staff

Assurance Tangibles Examples

We will follow this installation schedule:

WEEK	ACTIVITY
1	Analyze the communication needs
2	Design equipment configuration and functions Client review and approval
3-4	Install and test new system
5	Client employee training
6	Implement new system (on-site support)

Location Numbers	Installation Period
1 - 80	March 1 - August 30
81 - 160	September 1 - February 28
161 - 235	March 1 - August 30

Each phase of the project produces a deliverable for client review and approval:

PHASE	PHASE NAME	DELIVERABLE
I	*Functional Analysis*	*Functional Design Document*
II	*Detail Analysis*	*Module Design Documents*
III	*System Development*	*Alpha Test Results*
IV	*Pilot Testing*	*Pilot Test Results*
V	*Installation*	*Installation Exceptions Report Post-Installation Report*

QSI Instruments is an industry leader in the introduction of innovative predictive maintenance hardware and software. QSI allocates 12% of its annual budget for research and development activities. Over the past five years, the R&D Department has introduced fifteen new predictive maintenance products. Several of these products have received the Morris Baker National Maintenance Product Quality Award.

Other Buyer Assurance Options

Two options can also help you build assurance with the buyer:

- *past experience:* the buyer has had a previous and positive experience working with seller
- *references:* the proposal includes a list of the seller's past and current clients who will provide favorable references

Responsiveness to the Buyer

Writing a proposal involves a great amount of time, effort, and expense. Through your writing efforts and the delivery of an on-time, quality proposal, you satisfy another quality dimension:

Responsiveness: developed in a timely manner and demonstrates a
                   willingness to provide solutions for the buyer's needs
                   and wants and to help measure results

If auditing [analyzing] the buyer's operations and organization begins to
satisfy the empathy dimension, and providing logical and realistic
solutions satisfies the reliability dimension, then providing the buyer
with a timely and quality proposal that matches the buyer's needs and
wants satisfies the responsiveness dimension.

A sales professional can demonstrate responsiveness throughout the
sales cycle by nuturing the sales partnership. A sales professional can
also demonstrate responsiveness while enhancing the partnership by:

- educating the buyer [giving them new information and ideas]
- problem-solving [identifying innovative solutions]
- consulting with the internal champion
- providing a copy of your proposal for each of the buyer's team
  members
- formally presenting your proposal to a buying committee

The Proposal as a Tangible

The proposal itself satisfies a quality proposal dimension:

Tangible: enhances and supports the communication of your
                   message by its overall appearance, content and
                   organization

A proposal may be the first tangible a buyer gets from the seller. It
represents the seller's first implementation deliverable. The proposal also
represents an end-product of the sales partnership. It is concrete proof
that the sales partnership can make a difference. The proposal represents
proof that buyer and seller cooperation, collaboration, and consultation
can identify ways to make or save money for the buyer or add value.

Important Communications Vehicle

A top-notch proposal man not be enough to win the contract but a poor
quality proposal could lose it.

In many cases, a sales professional only works with one person in the buyer's organization to develop the proposal, an internal sponsor. The internal sponsor is integral to the sales partnership and is typically a member of a buying team, committee, or task force. The sales professional may never meet the other decision-makers. In these situations, the proposal's quality is as important as the sales professional's relationship with the internal sponsor.

Frequently the internal sponsor presents the proposal to the buying team or committee not the sales professional. In these situations, the proposal represents the seller. The sales professional must rely on the proposal's quality not the internal sponsor's presentation skills.

Therefore, a proposal may be the most important communications vehicle a seller can provide a buyer. It sells when the sales professional is not in front of the buyer.

Exhibit 7.1

Quality Proposal RATER

The following questionnaire is the *Quality Proposal RATER*. It is based on the five quality proposal dimensions presented earlier in this chapter. Use the RATER to evaluate a proposal's quality and effectiveness. Scoring the questions for each of the five dimensions will help you detect strengths and weaknesses. Score the questions using this scale:

5 - Excellent: clearly demonstrates outstanding quality

4 - Good: some minor weaknesses but clearly demonstrates high quality; minimum modifications needed to reach level 5

3 - Average: demonstrates adequate quality levels; needs substantial modifications to reach level 5

2 - Poor: barely meets minimum quality levels; needs major modifications to reach level 4 or 5

1 - Inadequate: does not meet quality level criteria — it is a disaster; recommend starting over

Reliability: reflects your [the seller's] ability to identify creative, dependable, and realistic solutions and strategies and match them to the buyer's needs and wants

Does the proposal:

___ 1. clearly artriculate proposed solutions and strategies?
___ 2. provide creative and innovative solutions and strategies for the buyer?
___ 3. present solutions and strategies appropriate for the buyer's business operation and organization?
___ 4. provide financial justifications that support the proposed solutions and strategies?
___ 5. provide references that support and reflect dependability?

___   RELIABILITY TOTAL

Assurance: builds the buyer's trust and confidence in your [the seller's] ability to deliver, implement, produce, service, and/or provide the benefits

Does the proposal:

___ 1. assure the buyer that the proposing organization has qualified, experienced, and competent leadership and staff?
___ 2. provide adequate specifications and/or benefits that substantiate ability and capability statements?
___ 3. present techniques, methodologies, or processes for assuring quality performance, e.g., deliverables, reviews, status reports, etc.?
___ 4. concisely and adequately define project or implementation roles and responsibilities?
___ 5. clearly identify and define all fees, prices, and expenses for completing the project?

___   ASSURANCE TOTAL

Tangibles: enhances and supports the communication of your [the seller's] message and invites readership by its overall appearance, content, and organization

Does the proposal:

_____ 1. provide a logical flow of information ideas and a sense of continuity for solving the buyer's business problems?

_____ 2. convert the intangible elements of the proposed solutions or strategies into tangibles, e.g., schedules, flow charts, staffing charts, etc.?

_____ 3. demonstrate high standards for excellence and quality in format, structure, and overall appearance?

_____ 4. provide positive indicators to differentiate the proposing organization from their competition?

_____ 5. contain a Letter of Transmittal, Executive Summary, Table of Contents, and supporting Appendices?

_____ TANGIBLES TOTAL

Empathy: conforms your [the seller's] thorough understanding of the buyer's business and their specific needs and wants

Does the proposal:
_____ 1. clearly identify the buyer's specific needs and wants?

_____ 2. demonstrate a thorough understanding of the buyer's business operations and organization?

_____ 3. provide solutions and strategies that fit within the buyer's business goals?

_____ 4. fulfill the buyer's original expectations?

_____ 5. identify and discuss financial and non-financial benefits in terms of their impact on the buyer's unique operation and organization?

_____ EMPATHY TOTAL

Responsiveness: developed in a timely manner and demonstrates a willingness to provide solutions for the buyer's needs and wants and to help measure results

___ 1. Did the proposal meet or beat the completion deadline established by the buyer or the proposing organization?
___ 2. Does the proposal reflect a genuine willingness to understand the buyer's business operations and organization and to provide viable and flexible solutions and strategies?
___ 3. Does the proposal reflect the proposing organization's willingness to work closely with the buyer by enthusiastically asking questions, gathering information, presenting options, and reviewing proposal drafts?
___ 4. Did the proposing organization thoroughly review the final proposal with the buyer and respond to their questions or clarify any outstanding issues and concerns?
___ 5. Are the proposed solutions or strategies within the buyer's budget and implementation timeframes?

___ RESPONSIVENESS TOTAL

Plot the five totals to visually illustrate the proposal's strengths and weaknesses relative to each quality dimension.

"Communicate unto the other guy that which you would want him to communicate unto you if your positions were reversed."

Aaron Goldman
CEO, The Macke Company, sign given to all managers

CHAPTER 8

◆

A QUALITY PROPOSAL:
RECOMMENDED STRUCTURE

"Opinion which is never organized is never heard."

Charles Merz
Journalist and publicist
The Great American Band Wagon
(The John Day Company, 1928)

Chapter Overview

By reading this chapter, you will review the similarities between proposals and sales presentations and understand how both must capture, focus, and maintain audience [reader] attention.

You will then learn about some important proposal writing guidelines:

- handling the reader with limited knowledge
- limiting the amount of detail
- not mixing information categories

Next you will be presented with:

- a recommended proposal structure
- suggestions for when and how to use appendices
- an example of an Executive Summary

Finally, you will review some ideas on proposal length and when to use a "Letter Proposal."

Written Sales Presentation

In many respects a proposal becomes your written sales presentation. Like sales presentations, successful and quality proposals require:

- planning and preparation — "Game Plan"
- a logical and systematic dissemination of information and ideas
- professional sales expertise
- an understanding of the intended audience
- convincing and persuasive reasons for the buyer to make a change or buy

Further, successful proposals, like successful presentations, must capture, focus, and hold the audience's interest. Therefore, a proposal should use many of the techniques employed in effective presentations:

- position the audience to be attracted and receptive
- provide a learning experience for the audience
- give the audience [reader] visual aids to direct their attention to critical elements or assist understanding
- introduce creative and innovative ideas and solutions to problems
- demonstrate the presenter's [writer's] and the organization's abilities, capabilities, and expertise

A successful proposal, or written sales presentation, must also demonstrate the five dimensions of quality: reliability, assurance, tangibles, empathy, and responsiveness.

Proposal Guidelines

You should follow several guidelines as you begin to structure your proposal:

Handle the reader with limited knowledge. As a writer, you must assume the reader may have limited knowledge of the topic. Therefore, your proposal must build the reader's knowledge by describing:

- the buyer's current situation
- your proposed solution or strategy
- how you or your organization will produce, deliver, or implement its services or products
- your proposed solutions or strategies: when and within what timeframe, with what resources, and what fees/prices

In other words, your proposal must become a logical and sequential learning mechanism for the reader.

Limit the amount of detail. You may remember an anecdote told about someone who bores you with too much detail, "When you ask him for the time, he tells you how to build a watch." Similarly, avoid putting too much or unnecessary detail in the main body of your proposal. It will bore and distract the reader. Rather:

- highlight important information in the main body
- use the appendices for detailed descriptions, calculations, specifications, etc.
- reference the appropriate appendices from within the proposal's main sections

For example, if your organization uses a complex, multi-phased methodology, do not put a five-page, detailed description of it in the section that discusses how you do business. Highlight its main phases and deliverables and direct the reader to an appendix for more detail.

Avoid mixing information categories. Format the proposal into a logical and sequential learning mechanism for the reader. The proposal's message should separate information into interrelated, logical categories such as:

- an overview of the buyer's current situation and their needs and wants
- a description of what you are proposing and why it will satisfy those needs and wants
- how you or your organization does business and why your methods will ensure delivery on the contract
- who will deliver on the contract, when it will happen, and how much it will cost

Categorizing information reduces the possibility of confusing, or worse, losing the interest of the reader. It also makes it easy for the reader to find information.

Recommended Proposal Structure

After reading the previous pages, you may have begun to envision our recommended proposal structure. We recommend that the proposal's main body contain four separate yet interrelated sections:

- Background Information
- Proposed Solution/Strategy
- Management/Production Methods
- Project or Implementation Plans

Further, a quality proposal must also include:

- an Executive Summary section
- a Table of Contents
- Appendices containing supporting detail and information

Chapters 10-13 will discuss each of the four main proposal sections and their recommended subsections in detail.

Interrelated Sections

A quality proposal separates information into interrelated categories. For example,

- The "Proposed Solution" section should describe how your proposed service(s) or product(s) benefits will satisfy the buyer's needs or wants identified in the "Background Information" section.
- The "Project/Implementation" section should describe when, who, and how much it will cost to deliver, produce, or implement your service or product. This section builds on the information presented in the previous section, "Management or Production Methods."

The following chart illustrates our recommended proposal structure and the interrelationships between the Executive Summary, four main sections, and appendices.

Exhibit 8.1

The Quality Proposal Structure

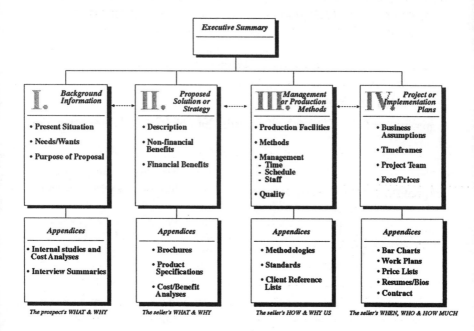

I. *Background Information*	**II.** *Proposed Solution or Strategy*	**III.** *Management or Production Methods*	**IV.** *Project or Implementation Plans*

• Present Situation
• Needs/Wants
• Purpose of Proposal
	• Description
	• Non-financial Benefits
	• Financial Benefits
		• Production Facilities
		• Methods
		• Management
		  - Time
		  - Schedule
		  - Staff
		• Quality
			• Business Assumptions
			• Timeframes
			• Project Team
			• Fees/Prices

Appendices • Internal studies and Cost Analyses • Interview Summaries	*Appendices* • Brochures • Product Specifications • Cost/Benefit Analyses	*Appendices* • Methodologies • Standards • Client Reference Lists	*Appendices* • Bar Charts • Work Plans • Price Lists • Resumes/Bios • Contract
The prospect's WHAT & WHY	*The seller's WHAT & WHY*	*The seller's HOW & WHY US*	*The seller's WHEN, WHO & HOW MUCH*

Appendices

Without appendices, your proposal could become a lengthy, unorganized aggregation of information. Too much detail could confuse the reader, or more importantly, disrupt the logical and systematic flow of ideas and information. Appendices provide a convenient place for supporting documentation. Use appendices for detailed reference material to:

- support summary financial calculations and statistics
- provide detailed product specifications
- list current and past clients
- describe and distinguish you or your staff's experience and capabilities
- support project/implementation timeframes and schedules

Chapter 14, will discuss appendices in more detail and provide examples of frequently used proposal appendices.

Executive Summary

The Executive Summary is the first and most important section of your proposal. This section's name identifies both its intended audience and purpose. It is written for senior management readers and provides a concise and condensed version of the entire proposal. The Executive Summary is the proposal in miniature.

Often, senior managers only read this section to get a high-level understanding of their organization's current situation and your proposed solution or strategy. They rely on their subordinates to verify your proposal's validity. Therefore, the Executive Summary section must demonstrate your best writing skills and capture the most important aspects of the entire proposal. It must clearly identify how your solution or strategy either makes or saves money for their organization — why they should sign your contract. The Executive Summary should stand alone as a proposal within a proposal.

Executive Summary Writing Tips

Here are some tips for writing the Executive Summary section:

Write it last. Some people suggest writing this section first to use as a basis for developing the actual proposal. Remember, this section is a summary of the proposal. If you write it first, what are you summarizing?

Include excerpts from each section. Reread each proposal section. Decide what is absolutely critical from each section to support and justify your solution or strategy, stimulate the reader, and describe the schedule and fees/costs of your solution or strategy.

Keep it short. You need to condense each proposal section into one or two paragraphs or bullet points for the Executive Summary. Some people set a one-page limit for an Executive Summary. There is no rule; however, a good range is two to three pages. If your Executive Summary is longer than three pages, you need to further condense it.

Executive Summary Example

The following illustrates an example of an effective Executive Summary.

Exhibit 8.2

EXECUTIVE SUMMARY

First State Bank of Texas (FSBT) employs 1360 part-time and full-time Tellers. With a turnover rate of 29%, FSBT must interview, hire, and educate nearly 400 new Tellers each year at a cost of $6,600 per Teller. Total annual new Teller costs are over $2,640,000. The purpose of this proposal is to show how employee selection testing and computer-aided interviewing can reduce these costs.

PreciseSelect, Incorporated (PSI) proposes FSBT implement its Automated Employee Selection System (AESS). This system contains two components:

Selection Testing
* *pre-interview tests delivered on a personal computer*
* *measured personality traits and attitudes, skills, and general learning and problem-solving abilities*

Computer-aided Interviewing
* *uses a personal computer to simulate critical work incidents*
* *provides the recruiter a method for observing and rating applicant responses*

AESS offers FSBT several benefits:

* *more effective, efficient, and consistent selection and hiring processes and procedures*
* *the selection of higher quality and more successful candidates*
* *reduced employment discrimination liability*

PSI's system will save the FSBT nearly $340,000 in its first year of operation. PSI's software license and implementation fees are $135,700. FSBT would realize a payback in less than five (5) months.

PSI's staff have used its six-phase methodology to implement AESS in over 150 client sites. This methodology provides a project management approach to:

- *develop employee profiles*
- *design and validate selection tests and interview scenarios*
- *implement AESS*

Preliminary estimates indicate PSI could implement AESS at FSBT in less than five months. Implementation activities could begin in mid-April; the system would be operational by early September.

PSI's fees for the project are:

• *AESS license fees*	*$ 75,000*
• *implementation fees*	*50,000*
• *travel-related expenses*	*6,000*
• *sales tax (software only)*	*4,700*
Total fees	*$135,700*

The annual software maintenance fees, including an on-site evaluation and re-validation process, is 20% of the current AESS license fee.

Proposal Length

The length of your proposal will depend upon the subject matter. Proposals for large construction projects or government procurement contracts often fill one or more large three-ring binders.

Before you begin writing, ask your internal sponsor or champion what his or her organization expects. Some organizations may have unwritten rules concerning acceptable length. For example, some buyers may expect a one-page Executive Summary with a five to ten page main body; all supporting information must be in appendices. Other buyers may want more detail in the main body and fewer appendices. In either case, the subject matter will still govern the overall proposal's length — however, your buyer's expectations will determine length and level of detail for the main proposal sections.

The Letter Proposal

Occasionally, you will find situations where a full proposal may be inappropriate for your proposed product, project, or product implementation. You will typically encounter these situations for:

- small or short-duration projects
- relatively low-cost products or product implementations

However, you may want or need to give your buyer a formal proposal. You can use a "Letter Proposal" for this purpose.

The proposal letter:

- is usually two to four pages long
- contains one or two paragraphs discussing the information normally contained in each of the four main proposal sections
- may have one or two attachments as replacements for a proposal's appendices
- optionally, may have a signature line for acceptance by the buyer

Note: You may want to eliminate the signature line and include a contract with your proposal letter.

Letter Proposal Example

The following example illustrates a Letter Proposal for consulting services.

Exhibit 8.3

W&T Associates, Inc.
5956 Bordeaux Lane, Suite 1500
Dallas, Texas 75220

April 23, 1993

Mr. James R. Wilson
Executive Vice President
First Western American Bankshares
1970 Chain Road
El Paso, Texas 72101

Dear Mr. Wilson:

Your bank faces tremendous employee education challenges with the introduction of totally new BA hardware and software. These challenges include:

- *identifying the scope and magnitude of the education effort*
- *estimating the educational program development effort and costs*
- *evaluating and recommending the correct instructional media*
- *evaluating and recommending internal and external development resources to form a project team*

Our proposed consulting engagement includes the following activities:

- *directing the efforts of your internal study team*
- *producing a BA Education System Recommendation Report*

I think our previous banking, computer-based training (CBT), and educational consulting background and experiences can provide a unique approach to your situation. Our method of operation for studies of this type will:

- *focus your staff's efforts to quickly gain an understanding in this area*
- *provide systematic techniques for gathering and analyzing information*
- *reduce the time necessary to study and evaluate the situation*
- *present a study document with conclusions and recommendations on which to base business decisions*

The following paragraphs outline our ideas for the study document, a workplan, and the proposed fees:

Proposed Deliverable	*The proposed deliverable includes, but is not limited to, the following sections:*

- *Executive Overview*
- *Analysis of Current Situation*
- *High-level Analysis of Branch Automation Instructional Needs*
- *Analysis of Appropriate Instructional Media Alternatives: Advantages and Disadvantages*
- *Evaluation of Internal Training Development Resources and Requirements*
- *Branch Automation Training Program Options: Benefits and Estimated Costs*
- *Conclusions and Recommendations*

Page 3

Engagement *The schedule for the proposed study is as follows:*
Schedule

Task/Activity	Time in Days Duration	Elapsed
Initial on-site activities:		
• *interviews/information gathering*	*3*	*3*
• *study team formation: roles and responsibilities*	*1*	*4*
• *outline the study document*	*1*	*5*
Study activities:		
• *develop study document*	*4*	*12*
Second on-site trip:		
• *review of draft document with study team*	*1*	*14*
• *identify conclusions and recommendations*	*1*	*15*
Finalize study document	*2*	*18*
Present, with your study team leader, the BA Education System Recommendation Report to BA Steering Committee	*1*	*21*

Engagement Fees *The fees for the proposed engagement are:*
- *$14,000, plus*
- *travel-related expenses*

Page 4

As we discussed, we are available to start the proposed engagement after May 15, 1993. If you agree with the proposed activities and tentative deliverable outline, please sign below.

Sincerely,   *Accepted for First Western American Bank:*

Mark H. Kinkaid
Principal

_____

James R. Wilson
Executive Vice President

"To communicate, put your thoughts in order; give them a purpose; use them to persuade, to instruct, to discover, to seduce."

William Safire
Columnist, *The New York Times*
Reader's Digest, December 1987

CHAPTER 9

$\blacklozenge$

TEAM WRITING THE PROPOSAL: RECOMMENDED STEPS

"Top management work is work for a team rather than one man."

Peter F. Drucker, 1983

Chapter Overview

In this chapter, you will study the recommended eight steps for proposal writing. Each step represents specific decisions, tasks, and activities for writing a quality proposal. The eight steps are:

1. Establish the proposal team
2. Outline the proposal (the "strawman proposal")
3. Review the outline with the buyer
4. Establish standards
5. Write the first draft
6. Edit the proposal
7. Write the Executive Summary
8. Review the first draft with the buyer

"Almost all quality improvement comes via simplification of design, manufacturing, layout, processes and procedures."

Tom Peters
Business Writer
Thriving on Chaos (Knopf, 1987)

Step 1: Establish the Team

The first and most important step in writing a quality proposal is establishing your proposal team. Two people make a team. Even if you are an independent consultant, you need at least one other proposal team member, a proofreader.

For most organizations, the size of a proposal team normally varies directly with the complexity and cost of the proposed solution. Having complete service or product knowledge does not necessarily qualify you to write a proposal. Further, you may not have the authority to make unilateral commitments for the organization as a whole. You may need to elicit input and cooperation from others, such as:

- production
- accounting
- operations
- customer service/support
- conversion support
- professional services

If you want to develop a quality, winning proposal team, follow these guidelines:

STEP	TASKS/ACTIVITIES
1.1	Define the team's purpose and the buyer's expectations
1.2	Clarify roles and responsibilities for each team member
1.3	Identify proposal writing timeframes and deadlines
1.4	Define steps, processes, and procedures

Step 2: Outline the Proposal

After completing the sales activities discussed in the previous chapters, you and your team are ready to outline the proposal. The outline becomes your "strawman proposal", because you will use it in the next step as a review document with your internal sponsor. This is a critical step in the writing process because it forces you and the team members to make major decisions concerning the proposal. It is no exaggeration to say that by the time you outline the proposal, you will have completed more than half of the work.

Follow these steps when outlining your proposal:

STEP	TASKS/ACTIVITIES
2.1	Define/title the main proposal sections
2.2	Define/title the subsections
2.3	For each subsection: • Write sentences describing the content or list the topics covered • Include financial summaries for the: - buyer's current costs - your proposed solution - other project-related costs
2.4	Identify and list the supporting materials to be included in the Appendices
2.5	Produce a draft of the outline
2.6	Review the outline for: • logical flow • proper sequence of ideas and arguments • inclusion of supporting data and information
2.7	In a team meeting, review and get agreement on the proposal outline
2.8	Make necessary changes and produce a working outline of the proposal

Step 3: Buyer Review

Before writing the proposal, use the outline as a "strawman proposal" to check validity and direction with your buyer. Schedule a proposal outline review meeting with your internal sponsor. This meeting will help insure that your final proposal meets the buyer's expectations — closes the "Expectations/Perceptions Gap."

Benefits of the "Strawman Proposal"

Reviewing the "strawman proposal" [proposal outline] with your buyer provides several benefits:

- insures that your final proposal will be customer-driven
- increases customer ownership of your proposed solutions
- demonstrates empathy and responsiveness
- continues to build buyer rapport and relationships
- improves the chances for writing a winning proposal

If the strawman proposal review meeting results in major revisions, meet with your proposal team to review the changes in detail. Use the meeting to assess the risk and impact these changes will have on your ability to meet the buyer's expectations. Further, you may want and need a second outline review meeting with your buyer before writing the proposal.

Step 4: Establish Proposal Standards

After your buyer and the proposal team approves your strawman proposal [outline], you are ready to start writing the final proposal. Before you begin, you need to establish several standards that you will follow throughout the proposal. This will save you and anyone who edits your proposal time and frustration. Making these decisions at this time will insure consistency and quality throughout the proposal. Some standards to consider include:

Capitalization. In addition to following the normal rules for capitalization, you will frequently encounter words, titles, and phrases that specifically relate to your buyer's or your organization. Decide how to deal with capitalization of these items. For example, capitalize the names of your buyer's and your organization's divisions and departments, products, methodologies, and systems:

• Southwest Division
• Accounting and Reporting Department
• Selection and Development Methodology
• Parts Inventory and Control System

Acronyms. Most organizations, including your own, normally substitute acronyms for the names or titles of products, procedures, and processes. Acronyms save time in communicating. However, to the reader with limited subject matter knowledge, the use of acronyms can be confusing and irritating. List the acronyms you plan to use in the proposal along with their proper names. Keep this list as a reference. For example:

CONCEPS: Computer On-line Customer Editing and Processing System

POS: Point of Sale

WBA: Western Builders Association

One rule to follow in your proposal: the *first* time you use an acronym, write out the acronym's full name or title followed by the acronym in parentheses, e.g., Affiliated Government Hospital Services (AFGS).

Format. Select the format you will follow throughout the proposal. Keep in mind a consistent format helps you avoid violating Deadly Mistake #4: Producing a proposal with little "drive-up" appeal. Ideally, you should develop a standard format that is used in all your proposals. Using a standard format will increase your proposal writing productivity and provide a consistent appearance for all your proposals.

Some things to consider when selecting or developing a format include:

- *Full text pages:* may be tiring to the reader and bury important points
- *Open text pages:* easier to read and allow for the organization and emphasis of critical information
- *Bullet items:* ideal for listing important points
- *Underlining:* perfect for identifying subsections and sub-points
- *Indentation:* excellent for easily locating subsections and sub-points
- *Flow charts:* simplifies complex processes or systems
- *Tables:* organizes information into logical and organized segments

The following pages contain several format examples for your review.

Exhibit 9.1

SECTION I: BACKGROUND INFORMATION

**Section
Overview**

*This proposal section discusses XYZ
Manufacturing's (XYZ) current inventory control
process. There are five major subsections:*

- *Current Operations*
- *Current Costs*
- *Identified Problems*
- *Impact on Quality*
- *Identified Needs*

**Current
Operation**

*XYZ's inventory control process involves three
components:*

*Hardware
(text)*

*Software
(text)*

*Procedures
(text)*

Exhibit 9.2

I: BACKGROUND INFORMATION

A. Section Overview

  *This proposal section discusses XYZ Manufacturing's (XYZ)
  current inventory control process. There are five major
  subsections:*

  1. Current Operations
  2. Current Costs
  3. Identified Problems
  4. Impact on Quality
  5. Identified Needs

B. Current Operation

  XYZ's inventory control process involves three components:

  1. Hardware
     (text)

  2. Software
     (text)

  3. Procedures
     (text)

Exhibit 9.3

SECTION I:

BACKGROUND INFORMATION

A. <u>Section Overview</u>

This proposal section discusses XYZ Manufacturing's (XYZ) current inventory control process. There are five major subsections:

- *Current Operations*
- *Current Costs*
- *Identified Problems*
- *Impact on Quality*
- *Identified Needs*

B. <u>Current Operation</u>

XYZ's inventory control process involves three components:

- *Hardware*
  (text)

- *Software*
  (text)

- *Procedures*
  (text)

Step 5: Write the First Draft

Start writing the first draft of the proposal using the outline as a roadmap. Write the proposal sections in sequence to develop a logical flow from one section to the next and to ensure consistency. By writing the proposal sections in order, you can build upon the information, ideas, and solutions presented in previous sections.

As you write the first draft, keep in mind these five dimensions of a quality proposal: reliability, assurance, tangibles, empathy, and responsiveness.

Step 6: Edit the Proposal

After you complete the first draft, you, and ideally your team, should edit the proposal to insure its quality. You may want to use the *Quality Proposal RATER* in Chapter 7 of this book as a guideline.

If you use a personal computer and word processing system, you have several technological tools to help:

Spell check: usually integrated into word processing systems
Grammar and punctuation check: several companies offer sophisticated software systems designed specifically for this purpose

Do not rely solely on these technological tools. Have several people proofread the first draft. If someone on your team or within your organization has an English or Journalism degree, appoint him or her as the official proposal proofreader. Remember, quality counts. Spelling and grammatical errors will distract readers from the content.

You may want to follow these editing steps:

EDIT STEP	TEAM MEMBER	ROLE/RESPONSIBILITY
6.1	Primary Writer	Edit each section as it is completed. Check for: • achieving proposal section objectives • continuity and flow from the previous section • accuracy of facts and calculations • correct spelling • grammar and punctuation
6.2	Primary Writer	Edit the complete proposal draft and review it for: • continuity and flow of the entire document • presence of supporting material in the appendices • accuracy of references to each appendix made from within the main proposal sections • compliance with the buyer's expectations
6.3	Proposal Team	Proofread and critique the draft proposal. Team members may want to use the Quality Proposal RATER as review guidelines. Approve the proposal draft.

6.4	Primary Writer	Enhance and change the proposal based upon the results of the team meeting. If significant enhancements or changes are made, consider repeating Editing Step #3.
6.5	Proposal Team	Hold a Proposal Team meeting to: • identify final changes • approve the proposal
6.6	Proofreader	Edit the proposal for spelling, grammar, writing style, and punctuation.
6.7	Primary Writer	Make changes based on the Proofreader's review and produce the final draft.

Step 7: Write the Executive Summary

As the last chapter stated, the Executive Summary is the most important section of your proposal. Its name identifies both its intended audience and purpose. When writing this section, use the guidelines presented in the previous chapter.

Step 8: Review with the Buyer

This eighth and last step is an important one to take. It is important because it provides another opportunity to get your internal sponsor's opinion or a "sanity check" on the overall proposal. This step should eliminate any surprises for your buyer and you or your organization.

If possible, schedule a meeting with your internal sponsor or champion to review the proposal draft. Make sure he or she has adequate time to read the proposal before the meeting. If your buyer is located halfway across the country, send him or her a copy to review. Schedule a time to review the proposal over the telephone. Make sure the review copy is marked "Draft Only".

If your internal sponsor recommends major changes, you may want to review them with your proposal team. You may also need to repeat Editing Step #8.

CHAPTER 9 CHECKLIST

___ 1. Proposal team selected.

___ 2. Team member roles and responsibilities defined.

___ 3. Proposal writing processes, procedures, deadlines, and timeframes established.

___ 4. "Strawman Proposal" [proposal outline] developed and reviewed with the team and buyer.

___ 5. Proposal standards established: capitalization, acronyms, and format.

___ 6. Proposal draft written, edited, reviewed, proof read, and approved by the team.

___ 7. Draft proposal produced.

___ 8. Executive Summary written.

___ 9. Proposal evaluated using the *Quality Proposal RATER.*

___10. Draft copy reviewed with internal sponsor.

"It's ... most profitable to work in teams where different investigators offer their particular expertise."

Rita Levi-Montalcine
Nobel laureate in physiology and medicine (Italy)
Omni, March, 1988

CHAPTER 10

◆

SECTION I: THE BUYER'S BUSINESS

"A problem that is located and identified is already half solved."

Bror R. Carlson
Director of Accounting
International Minerals & Chemicals Co.
Managing for Profit (IMAC, 1961)

Chapter Overview

By reading this chapter, you will:

- learn the purpose and importance of the first section of a quality proposal — the section in which you show your understanding of the buyer's business
- review the "Joe Friday Approach" to writing
- examine specifications and examples of recommended subsections:

   - Industry or Subject Matter Information
   - What and How
   - Problem or Opportunity — Needs and Wants
   - Financial Measures — Costs and Revenues
   - Purpose of the Proposal

Alternate Section Titles
- Background Information
- Proposal Background
- Present Method of Operations
- Present Operations
- Current Situation (or Operations)
- Statement of the Opportunity (or Problem)

Section Purpose
The primary purpose of this first proposal section is to prove to the buyer that you understand their business. This section must satisfy one quality proposal dimension:

Empathy: confirms your thorough understanding of the buyer's business and their specific needs and wants

Within this section you must:

- describe what your buyer is doing now and how they are doing it
- identify how much it costs your buyer to do it
- identify how much revenue and profit they make from doing it
- list the buyer's specific needs and wants

This section also has an important secondary purpose; it begins to build the credibility of your proposal and competence of your organization with the reader.

Joe Friday Approach
Use the "Joe Friday Approach" to write this section — "just the facts." Do not use this section as an opportunity to:

- criticize the buyer's operation
- illustrate the buyer's ignorance of available and obvious solutions

- expose the buyer's inability to make logical productivity and quality improvement changes
- exhibit the buyer's lack of expertise in your field

Industry or Subject Matter Information

Some of the proposal recipients and buying committee members may need basic industry or subject matter information. In other situations, the sales professional may be proposing that the buyer enter a new market or evaluate the use of a new technological innovation. In these cases, use an Industry Information subsection to:

- provide the reader with additional or needed information on which to base the buying decision
- show the buyer that you understand their business and can identify those aspects most important to the buying decision
- provide much needed background information to those readers with limited knowledge — insure all that the decision-makers are equally prepared to make an informed buying decision

Some salespeople incorrectly assume everyone has the same knowledge level about a particular aspect of the industry or business as he or she has. Remember, a sales professional can enhance the sales partnership by educating the buyer.

Describe the What and How

The proposed solution or strategy will impact your buyer's business. Use this subsection to show that you understand the buyer's current operations. Remember, you must understand the buyer's business before proposing a change. Use this subsection to describe the buyer's current:

- processes, procedures, and methods
- production and quality statistics
- staffing levels and turnover rates
- systems and equipment

What and How Example

An example of the what and how description for this subsection is given below. Note the level of detail it includes.

First State Bank of Texas (FSBT) employs 1,360 part-time and full-time Tellers in 189 branch offices. Even though FSBT enjoys an annual Teller turnover rate of 29%, each year the Bank must interview, hire, and educate 394 new Tellers.

All FSBT Tellers must have a High School education and pass the Bank's Math Skills Competency test. Other Teller profile elements may include:

• a college degree
• previous retail sales/customer service experience
• teller experience at another financial institution

The current FSBT selection process follows these seven steps for Tellers hired in metropolitan areas:

1. Applicants complete an application

2. Applications are forwarded to the Human Resources Division

3. A Recruiter reviews the applications and invites suitable applicants to interview

4. A Recruiter interviews selected applicants

5. If the interview is satisfactory, the applicant takes the math skills test

6. If the applicant passes the math skills test, he or she then interviews with the Branch Manager with the open position(s).

7. The Branch Manager makes the final decision.

The Teller selection, interviewing, and hiring processes at outlying Branches do not follow the above steps. Rather, Branch Managers select, interview, and hire their Branch's staff.

Business Problem or Opportunity—Needs and Wants

Before proposing a solution or strategy, you must first identify the business problem or opportunity facing the buyer. Although you may not title a subsection 'Business Problem' or 'Business Opportunity,' you must describe why the buyer should make a change.

Use this subsection to define the buyer's specific needs and wants as they relate to the solution or strategy you will present in the next proposal section. This subsection must set the stage for your proposed product or service. It should include:

- a statement of the business problem or opportunity
- the causes or reasons for the problem or opportunity
- a discussion of any plans or projects the buyer has for correcting the problem or capitalizing on the opportunity

Remember the "Joe Friday Approach" when writing this subsection — just the facts. Also remember, in a sales partnership, the buyer and seller jointly define the business problem or opportunity facing the buyer. Therefore, this subsection discusses the buyer's actual needs and wants not those developed by the seller to justify purchase of the proposed product or service.

Needs and Wants Examples

The following examples illustrate how to develop and support the needs and wants you identified with your buyer.

It is impossible to determine First State Bank of Texas' (FSBT's) exact Teller selection needs without a thorough and in-depth job analysis. However, conversations with the Human Resources Division staff and our experience in this area, point to several major criteria for employee success on the job:

- *cognitive ability*
- *dependability*
- *a customer service attitude*

Further, the ever-increasing complexity of employment law increases the need for FSBT to standardize its employment process to minimize Equal Employment liability. The need to standardize the selection processes will become more important if civil rights legislation pending in Congress is passed into law.

Acme Manufacturing uses three systems for purchasing, inventory control, and accounts payable. Staff from each operational department originally selected and installed their systems in 1982. Over the years, the three systems have been enhanced by Acme's data processing staff through:

- *new vendor releases*
- *internal custom changes*
- *interface programs*

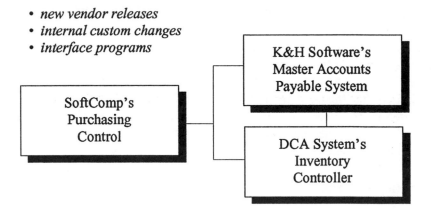

Based upon interviews conducted by our sales representative, Acme's staff from the three operational areas think their respective system provides adequate functions, features, and reporting. However, a recent operational review by Acme's internal auditors identified several problem areas:

- *difficulty in forwarding exceptions identified by one system to the other two systems*
- *nadequate and confusing exception audit trails between the three systems*

- *inability to match purchase orders, shipping receipts, and invoices on all purchases*

The audit staff thinks Acme needs to either rewrite the interface programs or purchase a new system that integrates these three functions.

Measure the Financial Impact of the Problem or Opportunity

Identify the buyer's current costs, expenses, and revenues related to the business problem or opportunity. If you are proposing the buyer resolve a problem, use this subsection to list current costs. Or, if you are proposing the buyer take advantage of a new business opportunity, list current revenue levels.

The financial measures used to help define the problem or opportunity will be the same measures you will use to calculate the financial benefits of your proposed solution. For example, if you use hourly production line downtime costs to measure a buyer's equipment maintenance problem, then you will use this financial measure as a basis for calculating the financial benefits of your proposed solution.

Keep several points in mind when measuring the fantail impact of the problem or opportunity:

- the financial information must be supplied by the buyer or mutually agreed to estimates — insure buyer ownership of the numbers
- if necessary, cite your sources in the proposal
- above all, insure your calculations are correct and easy to understand

Financial Measures—Cost/Revenue Examples

The following example illustrates how to measure current expenses for a particular operation. Note the example shows how the calculations were made.

First State Bank of Texas' (FSBT's) new Teller selection costs can vary depending upon:

- *internal cost accounting methods*
- *labor market conditions*
- *annual turnover rates and resulting volumes*

Most surveys place the average employment cost for each new hourly, clerical employee at $1,500. FSBT's Human Resources Division staff stated that this cost estimate is very reasonable for their operation.

Therefore, FSBT's total annual employment costs for new Tellers hired into metropolitan area Branches are:

• *Total number of new Tellers hired annually:*	*394*
• *Percentage of Tellers hired for metropolitan Branches:*	*80%*
• *Total number of new Tellers that go through the Human Resources Division's selection process (394 x 80%):*	*315*
• *Average employment cost per new Teller:*	*$1,500*

Total Annual Costs (315 x $1,500)   *$472,500*

The following example illustrates how to use the buyer's financial reports to develop financial measures in your proposal.

Based upon last year's Profit and Loss Statement, XYZ Manufacturing has fully loaded, annual personnel expenses of $1,500,000. The breakdown between management and production employees is:

- *Hourly Production*   *$950,000*
- *Management*   *$600,000*

The average, fully loaded cost per hour for production employees is:

- *Average number of production staff during the year:*   *37*
- *Average annual hours worked per production staff (50 weeks x 40 hrs/per week) - (7 holidays x 8 hrs/holiday) = (2000 -56)*   *1,944*
- *Total annual production hours (37 x 1,944):*   *71,928*
- *Average, fully loaded cost per hour for production employees ($950,000/71,928 hours): $13.21*

Explain the Proposal's Purpose

If you have done an adequate job describing the buyer's current operation, defining the problem or opportunity, and developing financial measures; then a logical case for your organization to propose a change exists. At this point, the buyer should clearly understand the business problem or opportunity facing the organization. However, you should use a "Purpose of the Proposal" subsection to:

- prepare the buyer for your proposed solution and strategy
- provide a transition to the next proposal section

Use one or two paragraphs to describe the purpose for your proposal. Do not provide detailed explanations of your solution or strategy at this time; save that for the next proposal section.

Purpose of The Proposal Examples

The following examples illustrate two effective "Purpose of This Proposal" subsections.

This proposal to First State Bank of Texas has two purposes, to:

* *show how the use of employee selection testing and computer-aided interviewing can:*
  - *reduce Teller turnover*
  - *reduce Teller selection and interview costs*
  - *improve the overall quality of newly hired Tellers*
  - *reduce job-employee mismatches*
  - *minimize Equal Employment liability*
* *present PreciseSelect, Incorporated's Automated Employee Selection System (AESS)*

The purpose of this proposal to Acme Manufacturing is threefold:

1. *Present K&H Software's Integrated Purchasing, Inventory Control, and Accounts Payable System (IPICAP).*
2. *Show how IPICAP can:*
   - *effectively and efficiently integrate purchasing, inventory and accounts payable data bases and thereby lower processing costs*
   - *satisfy the internal auditors' concerns for exception item processing and reporting*
   - *reduce the number of purchase order, shipping receipt, and invoice mismatches to further lower processing costs*
3. *Present K&H Software's new automated conversion and employee education program.*

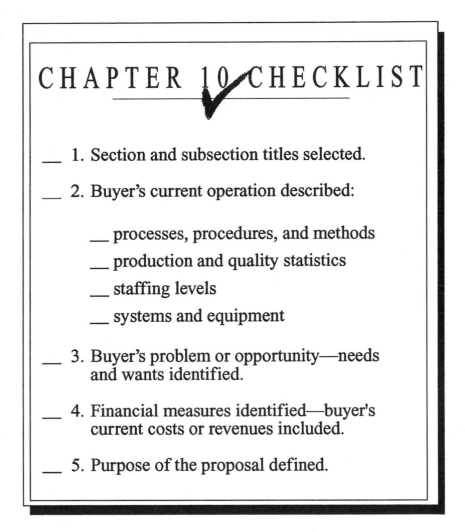

CHAPTER 10 CHECKLIST

___ 1. Section and subsection titles selected.

___ 2. Buyer's current operation described:

    ___ processes, procedures, and methods

    ___ production and quality statistics

    ___ staffing levels

    ___ systems and equipment

___ 3. Buyer's problem or opportunity—needs and wants identified.

___ 4. Financial measures identified—buyer's current costs or revenues included.

___ 5. Purpose of the proposal defined.

CHAPTER 11

◆

SECTION II: YOUR PROPOSED SOLUTION

"Don't forget that it [your product or service] is not differentiated until the customer understands the difference."

Tom Peters
Business Writer
Thriving On Chaos
(Knopf, 1987)

Chapter Overview

In this chapter, you will learn about the recommended second section of a quality proposal and its subsections:

- description
- non-financial benefits
- financial benefits

You will review this section's purposes, which are to:

- describe your proposed solution or strategy
- identify the proposed solution's or strategy's benefits
- support the Reliability and Tangibles dimensions of a quality proposal

Then, you will examine techniques and examples for describing your solution or strategy. You will learn why you must include the two benefit types, non-financial and financial, in your proposal. You will review several suggestions for measuring financial benefits and examine some examples.

Alternate Section Titles

- Proposed Solution
- " Project
- " System
- " Strategy
- " Product
- " Change
- " Engagement
- " Conversion

Section Purpose

The two primary purposes for this proposal section are to:

- describe your proposed solution or strategy
- present the non-financial [qualitative] and financial [quantitative] benefits of your proposed solution or strategy

The secondary purpose of this proposal section is to reflect your organization's ability to demonstrate two of the five dimensions of a quality proposal:

Reliability: reflects your ability to identify creative, dependable, and realistic solutions and strategies, and match them to the buyer's needs and wants

Tangibles: enhances and supports the communication of your message by its overall appearance, content, and organization

The Description

The first subsection should describe your proposed solution or strategy. This subsection should:

- detail what your service or product will do for the buyer
- include a brief description of the features, functions, and specifications of the product
- describe how the service or product will work in the buyer's unique environment

If you are proposing a complex solution or strategy, summarize its most important aspects and put the detail in an appendix. This subsection must:

- adequately describe your proposed solution or strategy
- avoid boring the reader with too much detail
- hold the reader's interest and keep him or her on track with your proposal's logic

Description Examples

The following examples illustrate how to write service and product descriptions. Note, neither description includes benefits, costs, or project/implementation timeframes.

Here is a service description example:

H&K Associates, Inc. (H&K) proposes ABC Software (ABC) contract H&K to assist them in developing an integrated strategic, business, and marketing plan. H&K's staff will perform the following:

Audit and Analyses
H&K consultants will conduct in-depth, internal and external audits. The audit will include but not be limited to:

- *Internal Audits:*
  - *management team interviews*
  - *key employee interviews*
  - *financial analyses*
  - *operations and functional analyses*
- *External Audits:*
  - *customer interviews*
  - *competitor analyses*

Creative Ideation

H&K will present their audit reports to selected members of the ABC organization. Following the presentation and in a team setting, the H&K consultants will conduct a creative "brain-storming" and "ideation" process. During this process the team members will identify innovative and practical ideas for ABC Software in critical operation, marketing, sales, and customer service areas. The ABC team will then arrange their ideas into major themes.

Strategic Theme Refinement

The H&K consultants and one or two of ABC's team members will lead the team through a theme refinement process that:

- *establishes five or six major themes for further development*
- *aligns each theme as a component of the integrated plan*

H&K will then assign two or more team members to each theme.

Critical Theme Development

Under H&K's guidance, sub-team members will develop each strategic theme as a project. The sub-team members will identify the critical attributes of their projects. Upon completion of these activities, a designated sub-team member will present his or her project or projects to the entire team.

Integrated Plan Development

This activity has two major sub-activities:

- *preliminary development of plan components by the team members*
- *final development of the integrated plan by the H&K consultants*

Here is a product description example:

PreciseSelect, Incorporated (PSI) proposes that First State Bank of Texas (FSBT) implement a new approach to Teller selection and interviewing. The proposed Automated Employee Selection System (AESS) for FSBT's Tellers will contain two components:

- *Selection Tests*
- *Computer-Aided Interviews*

Selection Tests

The first system component provides for a pre-interview test delivered on a personal computer. PSI will validate the test for FSBT's Teller population to measure:

- *personality traits and attitudes*
- *specific skills*
- *general learning and problem-solving abilities*

FSBT will use the pre-interview test results to:

- *provide data on which to base decisions for declining applicants*
- *select candidates for personal interviews*

Computer-Aided Interviews

The Computer-Aided Interviewing component provides an additional method by which FSBT can assess new Teller applicants. With the use of a personal computer, applicants are placed in an interactive situation which simulates critical work incidents. This component provides the Recruiter a method for rating applicant responses. It allows the Recruiter to observe intuitive responses to critical work situations.

Two Benefit Types

The next subsections should present the two types of benefits offered by your proposed solution or strategy.

- ***Non-financial:*** the *qualitative* traits, features, characteristics, and attributes of your solution or strategy—these are value-added benefits
- ***Financial:*** the *quantitative* advantages or improvements provided by your solution or strategy—your "walk the talk"

Financial [quantitative] benefits more often than non-financial [qualitative] benefits, determine whether the buyer signs your contract. This does not mean non-financial benefits are unimportant. Rather, it means your proposal must include both types.

Non-financial [Qualitative] Benefits Overview

Non-financial benefits identify the value-added aspects of your service or product. These are the benefits not easily measured in dollar terms that the buyer will gain by contracting with you or your organization. They represent benefits that are difficult to convert into tangibles—numbers that realistically support your solution. For example:

- increase or improve access to information for decision-making
- provide access to expertise, analysis techniques, and methodologies not readily available within the buyer's organization
- demonstrate an innovative, leading-edge approach to customer service

Feature - Benefit Conversion

By receiving your service or using your product the buyer will gain non-financial benefits. Your proposal should convert each of your service's or product's features into specific non-financial benefits for the buyer. For example:

- increasing or improving access to information for decision-making should lead to better decisions with the expectation that these decisions will improve revenues or reduce costs
- access to expertise, analysis techniques, and methodologies not readily available within the buyer's organization should:
  - assist the buyer's employees complete a project requiring a new discipline or technique
  - find the solution to a previously unsolvable problem
  - improve the way the buyer plans for change and thereby improve the overall quality of the changes themselves
- demonstrating an innovative, leading-edge approach to customer service should result in higher customer retention and the ability to attract new customers

Most buyers understand that your non-financial benefits will eventually result in longer-range financial benefits.

Non-financial Benefit Examples

The following examples illustrate how you might describe non-financial benefits:

Here is an example of non-financial benefits for consulting services:

ABC Software (ABC) will realize the following benefits by engaging H&K Associates, Inc. (H&K) to assist them in developing an integrated strategic, business, and marketing plan.

- *Unbiased analyses in the following areas on which to base plans and quality improvement projects:*
  - *business operations*
  - *marketing and sales programs*
  - *employee attitudes*
  - *competition*
  - *customers' attitudes on product and service*

- *A creative and integrated team-approach that will lead to identifying innovative and practical ideas for improving the quality of ABC's:*
  - *internal operations*
  - *marketing and sales programs for its XPAC and XPARK application software products*
  - *on-site and help desk customer service programs*
  - *XPAC and XPARK products and thereby its competitive position*
- *Establishment and development of five or six strategic themes as components of a totally integrated plan. Each strategic theme will become a project for ABC with:*
  - *identified tasks and activities*
  - *assigned roles and responsibilities*
  - *established timeframes*
- *An integrated strategic, business, and marketing plan that:*
  - *has employee support because it was developed with and through their cooperation*
  - *identifies five or six critical areas that will improve the overall quality of ABC's operations, marketing and sales programs, products, and customer service*
  - *identifies specific quality improvement projects for ABC to complete over the next 12-18 months*

Here is an example of non-financial or qualitative benefits from a software vendor:

First State Bank of Texas (FSBT) will realize the following non-financial benefits through implementation of PreciseSelect's Automated Employee Selection System (AESS):

- *more effective, efficient, and consistent selection and interview processes and procedures*
- *the selection of quality candidates*

- *a higher percentage of more successful and satisfied employees*
- *reduced employment discrimination liability through a statistically validated selection process*

The following table lists specific benefits by AESS component:

PROGRAM COMPONENT	NON-FINANCIAL BENEFITS
Selection Test	• *bases pre-interview selection decisions on unbiased, objective data* • *uses a pre-determined cutoff score to identify only those applicants best suited for the position* • *shows EEOC compliance because the test is based upon statistically validated data* • *provides supporting documentation for selection decisions*
Computer-Aided Interview	• *provides additional unbiased data on which to base hiring decisions* • *brings consistency and structure to the interview process* • *improves the effectiveness of the interview process – more successful employee-job matches* • *provides supporting documentation for hiring decisions – reduced liability*

Financial [Quantitative] Benefits Overview

As previously stated, financial or quantitative benefits represent your "walk the talk." If this proposal subsection does not demonstrate the financial viability of your proposed solution or strategy, your chances of getting a signed contract are slim. Financial benefits unquestionably must meet two Quality Proposal RATER dimensions:

Reliability: reflects your ability to identify creative, dependable, and realistic solutions and strategies, and match them to the buyer's needs and wants

Tangibles: enhances and supports the communication of your message by its overall appearance, content, and organization

The two most important words from these quality proposal dimensions are "realistic" and "support." Your proposal must provide realistic, financial benefits backed by indisputable, financial analyses.

Match Financial Benefits to Problem or Opportunity Measures

A winning proposal shows a buyer how to make or save money by solving a business problem or capitalizing on a business opportunity. The last chapter discussed how to identify the financial measures of the buyer's problem or opportunity in the first proposal section. Logically, the second proposal section, Proposed Solution, should use those financial measures as a basis for developing financial benefits. In other words, how ever you measure the problem or opportunity will determine how you measure the financial benefits of your proposed solution. For example

- If the buyer has been experiencing customer service errors and your proposed system reduces these errors, calculate the savings over the reasonable life of your system.

- If the buyer has production staffing problems during peak periods and your company provides temporary employees thereby reducing the need for full-time employees, calculate these cost-savings and its effect on expenses and profits.

The financial benefits you use in your proposal also may depend on the buyer's expectations. For example

- If your buyer expects that your service will shorten their project time, measure the cost of your services against the delayed start of the project and the cost of recruiting and hiring an employee who possesses your expertise.
- If your buyer expects to add new customers by implementing your product, calculate the expected increased revenue and profits.

Remember, your proposal must show the buyer how your service or product provides a business solution—makes or saves money.

Measuring Financial Benefits

Besides matching financial benefits to the way the buyer measures the problem or opportunity, you may need to use one of the following standard financial calculations.

Cost savings or increased revenues converted into profit contribution. If your buyer thinks in millions of dollars, it may be difficult to convince them a small decrease in cost per unit makes a big difference. However, if you convert the per unit cost savings to bottom-line profits, your proposed solution should have more impact. For example, if your solution reduces costs by $3.50 per unit and the buyer sells 300,000 units per year, you could use this type of example:

TOTAL COST SAVINGS	PROFIT MARGIN	SAVINGS EQUAL TO PROFIT ON REVENUES OF:
$1,050,000	20%	$ 5,250,000
$1,050,000	15%	$ 7,000,000
$1,050,000	10%	$10,500,000

Years to Payback or Payback. Measure the years needed for the buyer to recover the investment. You will need to identify associated savings or revenue enhancements.

$$\frac{\text{Cost of the Proposed Solution}}{\text{Buyer's Total Annual Savings or Revenue}} = \text{Years to Payback}$$

For example: You propose that the buyer organization eliminate specific classroom instruction programs by converting to a computer-based training (CBT) system and writing CBT courses. Your buyer currently spends $685,000 per year to provide employee training on its internal system. Your proposed CBT solution would cost $825,000 to implement and would save $500,000 each year in related training expenses. The Payback would be $825,000 divided by the $500,000 annual savings or 1.65 years.

Return on Investment (ROI). Measure the buyer's return on their investment.

$$\frac{\text{Average Annual Net Pre-tax Income}}{\text{Total Solution Cost}} = \text{ROI}$$

For example: You estimate your proposed system will generate $32,500 dollars of net pre-tax income for your buyer each year for the next three years. Total estimated costs of your system, including all incremental and operating costs, over the three year period are $55,470. The ROI for your solution is:

$$\frac{\$32,500}{\$55,470} = 58.6\%$$

Earnings per Share. Senior managers of most publicly held companies like to know the effects of purchases and acquisitions in terms of *earnings per share*. This financial measure directly equates with the trading price of a share of stock through the Price-Earnings (PE) Ratio, e.g., a stock with a PE Ratio of 20 and earnings per share of $1.00 will trade for $20.00.

Since senior managers are measured by their ability to increase earnings, they like to see what impact major proposals will have on the bottom line. And, since many senior managers also own stock in their companies, they can easily see how the proposal will affect their personal net worth.

$$\frac{\text{Average Annual Savings}}{\text{Number of Outstanding Shares}} = \text{[Affect on]}\ \text{Earnings per Share}$$

For example: If your proposed solution will save the buyer $2,000,000 each year and the buyer has 100 million outstanding shares, the increased earnings per share would be $2 million divided by 100 million shares or $0.02 per share.

If one of the decision makers owned 100,000 shares and the stock had a PE Ratio of 25, the buy decision could mean a $50,000 increase in personal net worth [$0.02 per share times a PE Ratio of 25 times 100,000 shares equals $50,000].

Financial Benefit Examples

The following examples illustrate how you can develop realistic financial benefits to support your proposed solution. Notice the level of detail and the use of buyer information.

Here is an example of financial benefits for a consulting services firm:

Based upon conversations with ABC Software's (ABC) senior management, H&K Associates, Incorporated (H&K) expects to reduce ABC's annual planning cycles and related costs. Using H&K's Integrated Strategic, Business, and Marketing Planning Methodology, ABC will simultaneously develop its 1994 strategic, business, and marketing plans.

The following table compares 1993 actual planning costs to the expected 1994 costs:

| PLAN TYPE | ACTUAL 1993 | | ESTIMATED 1994 | |
	TIME	COST	TIME	COST
Strategic	*2 mo.*	*$25M*	*1 mo.*	*$10M*
Business	*4 mo.*	*$28M*	*1 mo.*	*$ 7M*
Marketing	*3 mo.*	*$24M*	*1 mo.*	*$ 8M*
TOTALS	*9 mo.*	*$77M*	*3 mo.*	*$25M*

NOTE: Time and cost estimates are based upon actual 1993 statistics. Time is stated in person-months. Costs reflect average, fully-loaded costs for each representative area.

H&K's total fees to develop ABC's 1994 integrated strategic, business, and marketing plan are $30,000 (see Section IV for more detail)

Total 1994 planning costs for ABC are estimated at:

• *Internal ABC costs:*	*$25,000*
• *H&K fees:*	*$30,000*
Total Estimated 1994 Planning Costs	*$55,000*

Based upon last year's costs of $77,000, ABC could expect to reduce 1994 planning costs by $22,000 or 28.8%.

Here is an example of financial benefits for a software product:

The use of PreciseSelect, Incorporated's (PSI) Automated Employee Selection System (AESS) will provide financial benefits in several areas:

• reduced selection and interviewing costs
• reduced turnover due to employee-job mismatches

Selection and Interviewing Savings
The use of pre-interview Selection Testing will reduce the number of personal interviews First State Bank of Texas (FSBT) will need to conduct by an estimated 30% through the:

• elimination of unqualified candidates
• increased quality of candidates interviewed

Based upon our analysis, we determined FSBT interviews five (5) candidates for every one (1) Teller hired. The cost to select, interview, and hire one Teller is $1,500. Therefore, FSBT will reduce its overall costs by 30% or $450 for each Teller hired ($1,500 x 30%) = $450).

FSBT will realize total annual savings of:

- *Total number of new Tellers hired annually:*   *394*
- *Percentage of Tellers hired for metropolitan Branches:*   *80%*
- *Total number of new Tellers that go through the Human Resources Division selection process:*   *315*
- *Estimated average employment cost savings per Teller:*   *$450*

Estimated Total Annual Selection and
Interview Savings (315 Tellers x $450)   *$141,750*

Savings from Reduced Turnover

We estimate the use of both Pre-interview Selection Testing and Computer-Aided Interviewing will reduce Teller turnover by 10% for Tellers hired in metropolitan areas. Since the current annual turnover rate is 29%, we estimate through the use of AESS, FSBT will lower this rate to 26%.

Reducing the turnover rate will result in additional savings by decreasing the number of new Tellers the Bank hires each year. As a result, FSBT will lower:

- *selection, interviewing, and hiring costs (currently $1,500 per new Teller; projected to decrease to $1,050 with PSI's AESS)*
- *total training costs (estimated at $5,130 per Teller by FSBT's Accounting Department)*

FSBT will realize total annual savings of:

- *Total number of new Tellers hired annually at current 29% turnover rate*   *394*
- *Percentage of Tellers hired for metropolitan Branches:*   *80%*
- *Total number of new Tellers that go through the Human Resource Division's selection process and the FSBT Teller Program:*   *315*

- *Total number of new Tellers hired annually at the
  new turnover rate of 26% (metropolitan areas only):*   *283*
- *Reduced number of new Tellers hired and trained:*   *32*
- *Hiring and training cost per new Teller
  ($1,050 + $5,130):*   *$6,180*

*Estimated Total Annual Savings from Reduced
Turnover (32 Tellers x $6,180)*   *$197,760*

*The total license and implementation fees for PreciseSelect's AESS
is $135,700. (see Section IV for more details)*

PreciseSelect estimates FSBT will realize a payback of 0.40 years:

- *Estimated Total Annual Selection and Interview
  Savings:*   *$141,750*
- *Estimated Total Annual Savings from Reduced
  Turnover:*   *197,760*

Estimated Total Annual Savings: *$339,510*

$$\frac{\$135,700 \text{ AESS license fee}}{\$339,510 \text{ savings per year}} = 0.40 \text{ years}$$

"The real issue is value, not price."

Robert T. Lindgren
Cross & Trecker Corp.
Harvard Business Review, March/April 1988

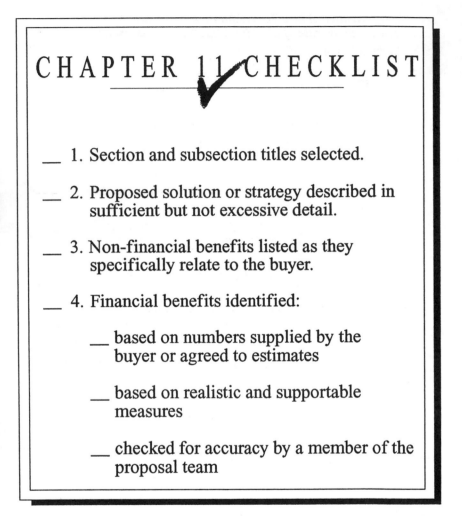

CHAPTER 11 CHECKLIST

___ 1. Section and subsection titles selected.

___ 2. Proposed solution or strategy described in sufficient but not excessive detail.

___ 3. Non-financial benefits listed as they specifically relate to the buyer.

___ 4. Financial benefits identified:

    ___ based on numbers supplied by the buyer or agreed to estimates

    ___ based on realistic and supportable measures

    ___ checked for accuracy by a member of the proposal team

CHAPTER 12

$\blacklozenge$

SECTION III: YOUR PRODUCTION, PROJECT, OR IMPLEMENTATION

"One critical source of knowledge is an understanding of how your organization formulates policies."

Dale E. Zand
New York University
Information, Organization, and Power
(McGraw-Hill, 1981)

Chapter Overview

By reading this chapter, you will learn about an often overlooked proposal section — a description of your or your organization's approach to production, projects, or implementations. You will discover ways to:

- describe how you or your organization operates and will perform on the contract
- build credibility and reduce risk
- satisfy the Assurance and Tangible quality dimensions

Next, you will review some ideas for how this section may vary depending upon your business and reexamine the concept of "Assurance Tangibles". You will understand why this proposal section needs to include three Assurance Tangibles:

- deliverables
- signoffs
- facilities

Finally, you will study the following recommended proposal subsections and examples of each:

- Production/Servicing Facilities
- Project/Implementation Management
- Quality
- Schedule Basis and Assumptions
- Budget Considerations
- Staff
- Status Reports
- "Why Us"

Alternate Section Titles
- Production Management
- Project Management
- Implementation Management
- Product Implementation
- Project Methodology
- Engagement Management
- Services Management

Section Purpose
The primary purpose of this third proposal section is to describe how you or your organization operates and plans to perform on the contract.

Within this section, you must:

- build credibility with your buyer
- reduce the perceived risk your buyer may have in dealing with you or your organization
- differentiate yourself or your organization from the competition

This section also helps satisfy two quality dimensions:

Assurance: builds the buyer's trust and confidence in your ability to deliver, implement, produce, service, and/or provide the benefits

Tangibles: enhances and supports the communication of your message and invites readership by its overall appearance, content, and organization

To satisfy the Assurance and Tangible dimensions, this section must indicate your ability and capability to:

- produce the product
- provide your services to the buyer
- implement your product in the buyer's organization
- deliver the benefits described in the proposal
- provide ongoing customer service

The section also must describe your production capabilities and project or implementation plans in ample detail to satisfy any buyer's concerns in this area.

Section Variations and Options

The contents of this section will vary depending upon your organization and what you are selling. *Consultants* and consulting services organizations should describe how they address:

- project management
- quality
- schedules
- staffing
- status reports

Service providers should describe:

- facilities and equipment
- customer service and training resources
- conversion management and techniques
- service quality
- staffing

Manufacturers should describe:

- facilities and equipment
- production capacities
- design and development techniques
- product quality
- staffing

Note: If your organization fits into two or more of the above categories, your proposal will need to include subsections from each of the above categories. For example, a software vendor that also provides consulting services might describe its:

- design and development techniques
- staffing (development, consulting, customer service, and training)
- development facilities and equipment
- customer service and training resources
- product quality
- service quality
- project management techniques

Working with your internal sponsor should help you define buyer expectations which will help you decide what to include in this section. He or she should know what the buyer organization wants to assure performance on the contract.

Assurance Tangibles

An earlier chapter introduced the concept of "Assurance Tangibles." Assurance Tangibles convert the intangible elements of your production, project, or implementation into tangibles. They give the buyer confidence in your ability to deliver on the contract. This section of the proposal requires inclusion of three of the five Assurance Tangibles:

Deliverables: Documents, events, or products that record completion of tasks and activities.

Signoffs: Opportunities throughout your project or implementation for your buyer to approve your deliverables.

Facilities: Descriptions of your production and support facilities, equipment, and staff.

Production/Servicing/Facilities Subsection Examples

If you sell products or services, you must describe your production or servicing facilities. This will reassure the buyer that you have the capacity to deliver.

The following example shows how a boat trailer manufacturer might describe its production capabilities.

In 1989, Towrite Trailers moved into their new plant in Canton, Texas. This 200,000 square foot facility incorporates the:

- *most recent advances in steel and aluminum extrusion machinery*
- *latest automation and robotic production tools and techniques*
- *premium painting and finishing equipment*

Towrite employs a staff of 125 production associates in a two-shift operation. Weekly production capabilities range from 150 to 175 trailers depending upon size and configuration. See Appendix F for more information on our production facilities.

The following example illustrates how a data processing organization might describe its servicing capabilities.

Federated Computer Services (FCS) provides data processing and operations support services to 135 financial institutions in five southwestern states. FCS' main data center in Tulsa, Oklahoma, continually enhances its data processing and telecommunications facilities and equipment. The Production Planning Department constantly:

- *monitors capacity and operational requirements*
- *evaluates new equipment capabilities*

This ensures that FCS maintains state-of-the-science equipment and the highest levels of quality service for its customers.

In addition to its Tulsa center, FCS has four remote data centers to provide:

- *item capture processing and report production functions*
- *readily accessible customer service and support functions*

See Appendix G for a detailed description of FCS' data center facilities.

Project/Implementation Management Subsection

The time required to complete most consulting engagements and many product and service implementations ranges from one week to several years. You need to assure your buyer that you or your organization have the abilities and capabilities to manage resources, activities, logistics, etc., throughout the project or implementation period.

Therefore, your proposal must provide these assurances in sufficient detail to satisfy the buyer's concerns — minimize the perceived risks. Using basic project management principles in your business and incorporating them in your proposal can greatly enhance your chances of getting the contract.

Project/Implementation Management Examples

The following example illustrates how a software and professional services vendor might describe its project management principles.

The success of a project depends not only on the use of a development methodology but also on the skilled management of the project. PreciseSelect, Incorporated uses a project management methodology for on time and within budget development and implementation.

Project Management Functions
Project management deals with three aspects of development:

- *the **quality** of the tests and scenarios*
- *the project **schedule,** and*
- *the project **budget***

All project phases require a cooperative effort between the client and PreciseSelect. A benefit of effective project management is timely communication between both organizations. This ensures that all activities are the result of agreements based on a clear understanding of the nature and scope of each project phase.

Deliverables
The principle deliverables of the project are the final versions of the selection tests and interview scenarios. PreciseSelect produces interim deliverables in each phase, as described in Appendix C. These interim deliverables provide for review of the project's progress and approval of the test and scenario designs/contents at various stages of the project.

The following table identifies the phases PreciseSelect will use for the First State Bank of Texas' project (see Appendix C for more detail):

PHASE	PHASE NAME	DELIVERABLE
1	*Analysis & Design*	*Project Definition Document*
2	*Detail Design*	• *Test Module Design Documents* • *Interview Scenario Design Documents*
3	*Development*	• *Alpha-tested selection tests and interview scenarios*
4	*Pilot Testing*	*Validated test and scenario results*
5	*Implementation*	*AESS run reports*
6	*Operation*	*Post-project Review Report*

Often times manufacturers use a project management approach to design and develop custom products. The following example illustrates how a boat trailer manufacturer might incorporate its custom product development techniques in a proposal to a boat builder.

Besides building its own line of boat trailers, Towrite Trailers, over the last six years, has manufactured custom boat trailers for several major boat manufacturers. Based upon its experiences, Towrite has developed a custom trailer design process to ensure:

- *proper hull support*
- *loading efficiency*
- *optimized balance and tongue weight*
- *visual aesthetics*

Towrite's custom trailer design process involves four critical steps:

1. *Design and engineering*
2. *Prototype development*
3. *Testing*
4. *Quality standards development*

Throughout this phase-limited process, our engineering staff works closely with the boat builder's staff to validate trailer designs and specifications. Towrite's process requires review and approval of each step's documents/deliverables before initiating the following step's activities. See Appendix D for more details on this process

Quality Subsection

Everyone expects quality in the products and services they buy. Therefore, the proposal needs to identify your or your organization's attitudes and considerations for ensuring quality. Again, what you sell dictates what you must include in this subsection.

- Consultants and consulting services organizations should discuss quality in terms of its relative importance to the project's budget and schedule and how quality is maintained throughout the engagement.
- Service providers should describe their organization's commitment to providing quality customer service. This is an ideal place for an organization's quality customer service mission statement.
- Manufacturers should describe their quality standards and processes. Again, this is an ideal place to include a quality mission statement.

Quality Examples

The following examples illustrate quality subsections for several different types of organizations.

Here is an example of how a consulting services organization providing software development services might describe their concern for quality:

> *Of the three aspects of the project (quality, schedule, budget), quality is the one aspect that remains with the Automated Employee Selection System as long as First State Bank of Texas (FSBT) uses it. For that reason, PreciseSelect, Incorporated (PSI) pays extraordinary attention to quality, without sacrificing the schedule and budget. However, we do recognize that problems can arise in meeting expectations and schedules during a project. If problems do occur, we will work closely with your staff to resolve them in a timely manner.*
>
> *Since starting the company in 1983, PSI's management has instituted quality standards in its software design and implementation engagements. PSI enjoys an excellent reputation with our past and present clients. Appendix C lists our clients; we readily encourage you to use them as references.*

This is Hart Graphics' "Quality Assurance" statement. Hart Graphics printed this book.

> *At Hart Graphics we are pledged to work harder than ever to provide you with the highest quality product our industry has to offer. In order to achieve this goal, we have a Quality Assurance Department made up of professional experts. Using Statistical Process Control we apply numerous measurements to ensure you the highest quality product. We use state-of-the-art process control equipment on our web presses in order to provide consistent and accurate products. Additionally we use densitometers, page-pull tests, 5000K lights, flex tests, and the Sutherland rub test for measuring empirical variables. Your job is thoroughly inspected*

throughout each phase of our manufacturing process. From in-coming materials testing to stringent quality assurance measures in kitting and assembly, we've got you covered. For your convenience our bar-code electronic job-tracking system allows for quick response on the status of your job at any point during the manufacturing process.

Here is an example of how a manufacturer might describe its quality processes and standards in a proposal:

In 1988, the senior management of Towrite Trailers recognized the need to improve quality — transform the way the company did business. As a result, Towrite initiated an ongoing, Total Quality Management (TQM) campaign. Because of this campaign, Towrite constantly improves its manufacturing processes and systems with the goal to build the highest quality boat trailers available in the country.

Early in our TQM campaign, we recognized that quality begins with raw materials. Therefore we have established long-term, single source relationships with all of our suppliers. We work closely with our suppliers to:

• minimize incoming raw materials variations
• constantly improve the quality of the trailers' components

Towrite also recognized the need to maintain quality manufacturing standards. In 1988, we implemented a statistical quality control process to replace an outmoded inspection process. In the last two years, the quality of our trailers has increased to the point where we received the American Boating Industry Manufacturer's Award for Excellence in 1990.

*Appendix J of this proposal contains a reprint of a **Manufacturers' Monthly** (magazine) article describing Towrite's TQM campaign.*

Schedule Basis Subsection

If your buyer has concerns regarding your proposed production, project, or implementation schedule, use this subsection in your proposal to confirm your understanding of the schedule's importance to the buyer. Also use the subsection to describe your basis for scheduling, such as:

- past experience
- preliminary reviews
- buyer provided information
- buyer staff and resources
- a stable system or production process
- a trained and skilled workforce
- readily available materials

Remember, this section of the proposal must assure the buyer that you can deliver on the contract. Describing why and how you or your organization approach scheduling certainly adds to the Assurance dimension.

Schedule Basis Examples

The following examples show how a "Schedule Basis" subsection in your proposal can help assure your buyer that you or your organization can meet the proposed timeframes and milestones.

Here is an example of how a software and professional services vendor could describe how it schedules:

> *PreciseSelect, Incorporated (PSI) understands First State Bank of Texas' (FSBT) desire and need to implement new selection and interview processes as soon as possible. PSI's Automated Employee Selection System (AESS) is very stable. This permits the establishment of predictable project schedules. If a scheduling problem does occur during development, PSI will make every effort to minimize its impact on the schedule.*

PSI bases the timeframe for this project on:

- the preliminary review of the proposed tests and interview scenarios
- its development experience
- information gathered during conversations with FSBT staff

Based upon these factors, PSI estimated the scope of the project. Keep in mind that these estimates may require some revision based on the findings of the first project phase.

PSI assumed the following when preparing the schedule:

Availability of FSBT Staff and Resources
PSI will need FSBT staff and resources for the project:

- Branch Operation Division staff to support Teller job analysis
- Human Resources Division staff to participate in Teller profiling tasks
- Tellers for validity testing
- FSBT's Teller Policy and Procedure Manual

PSI also requests FSBT designate a Project Coordinator to facilitate communication between organizations.

Prompt Review and Approval Cycles
PSI assumes that FSBT's project staff will return materials sent for review and approval within five (5) working days. If the FSBT project staff is not certain that they can provide this turnaround time, they will need to let us know during the first project phase. This will allow us an opportunity to adjust the schedule accordingly.

Here is a production scheduling example for a manufacturer:

When a boat builder decides to package their boats with custom trailers, they add another variable to their product delivery schedule. Towrite Trailers recognizes the importance of matching boat and trailer production schedules.

To coordinate scheduling, Towrite allows boat builders access to their Production Management System (PMS). As soon as a boat builder establishes their production schedule, they can input trailer production requirements into PMS using and on-line terminal (or personal computer with a modem and emulator software).

Towrite can build a custom trailer within five (5) to seven (7) working days after receiving an order because of its:

- *just-in-time production processes and systems*
- *automated production facilities*
- *skilled and stable workforce*

Shipping to most locations takes an additional three (3) to five (5) days. Since Sea Sled Boats schedules model production runs four (4) weeks in advance, our trailers would arrive in time to load matching boats directly from your assembly line.

Budget Considerations Subsection

Your proposal should assure your buyer that you or your organization can produce, service, or implement within the proposed budget. Depending upon what you are proposing, you may have to discuss how you or your organization will hold to the project's or product implementation's budget or adjust prices or fees over the term of the contract.

Budget Considerations Examples

The following two examples illustrate budget subsections:

This is an example of a Budget Considerations subsection for a software and professional services vendor:

Project Budget

Adherence to the project's budget is primarily PreciseSelect, Incorporated's (PSI) responsibility. PSI is responsible for the accuracy of the estimated expenditures of time and resources required to produce the employee selection tests and computer-aided interview scenarios for First State Bank of Texas (FSBT).

There are circumstances in which PSI may come to you and ask for a change in budget. If delays or rewrites occur because of FSBT-requested changes, PSI's Project Manager will prepare and send your Project Coordinator a Budget Change Notice showing the nature and scope of the change and asking for your approval. PSI will not proceed with changes until we receive FSBT approval.

Revisions late in the development cycle also require a budget change. If FSBT's project staff decides during the development phase that the test questions or interview scenarios are not what they want, the PSI Project Manager will most likely prepare a Budget Change Notice before making the changes. PSI records and revises tests and scenarios based upon review changes identified in the first or second phases of the project. Later revisions are more expensive and time-consuming than earlier revisions.

Here is an example of how a manufacturer might assure a buyer about future costs:

The ability to set and maintain competitive custom trailer prices throughout the contract is important to any boat builder. Over the last three years, Towrite Trailers' long-term, single source supplier relationships have minimized price increases. Our average price increases over the last three years have been:

- *1988: 4.25%*
- *1989: 3.75%*
- *1990: 3.20%*

Many external factors can affect our future material costs. However, Towrite is confident in its ability to maintain annual price increase to less than 3.5% over the next two years.

Staffing Subsection

Unless you are an independent consultant who will personally provide all the proposed services, your proposal should discuss plans for staffing the project or implementation. If your proposal involves a critical design and production staff, it should discuss how your organization will use this staff to execute the contract.

Staffing Examples

The following examples show how to include staff information in this section. Note: You might use this subsection to reference an Appendix.

This is an example of how a service provider could write the "Staffing" subsection:

Federated Computer Systems (FCS) will use their Client Conversion Team to provide an efficient and effective transition from your current service bureau. Client Conversion Team members must meet rigid qualifications:

- *a minimum of three (3) years experience at FCS in either Client Services or Application Maintenance*
- *successful completion of all courses offered by the FCS University*
- *a recommendation from their immediate supervisor for team consideration*

FCS has Client Conversion Teams in each of its five regions. The team from your region will manage your financial institution's conversion. However, in some situations, team members from another region may assist on your conversion.

Here is an example for a software and professional services vendor to describe project staffing:

On most Automated Employee Selection System (AESS) projects, PreciseSelect, Incorporated (PSI) uses only PSI consultants from its Professional Services Department. However, on some projects, we may use qualified Industrial Psychologists when a project requires specific expertise. This assures the best resources for your project.

Status Reports Subsection

Reporting status is important, whether to periodically advise the buyer on your project/implementation activities or to report actual production statistics. This often overlooked proposal subsection assures your buyer that you or your organization plan to keep them informed and understand the importance of ongoing communications.

Your proposal should describe how, how often, and to whom you will send status reports, production statistics, or hold progress meetings.

Status Reports Examples

The following examples present Status Report subsections.

This is an example for a software and professional services vendor to use for the Status Report subsection:

PreciseSelect, Incorporated's Project Manager issues Project Status Reports on a monthly basis or whenever there is a scheduled project status meeting. The purposes for the Project Status Report are:

- *to keep FSBT's and PSI's staff and management informed on all aspects of the project*
- *to officially record completion of phase activities and project milestones*

Here is a Status Report subsection example for a manufacturer:

Towrite Trailers wants to keep its custom trailer customers informed throughout the:

- *Custom trailer design process*
- *Contract term*

Custom trailer design process
Our Senior Engineer, John Daniels, who has been with Towrite since 1976, is the Project Manager for all custom design projects we undertake with boat builders. Mr. Daniels will issue status reports at the completion of each design step.

Contract term
Throughout the three year contact period, your Client Representative will review production statistics on a bimonthly basis at your offices. Ms. Ruth M. Burdick will be assigned as your Client Representative. Ms. Burdick will use several Client Production Statistics Reports produced by our Production Management System for the reviews.

The "Why Us?" Subsection

After thoroughly describing how you or your organization operates, you may think it is obvious to the buyer why they should sign your contract. Do not make this fatal assumption. Use this last subsection to restate and link the service or product benefits and your quality approach within your business

Some proposal writers think this subsection reflects an egocentric attitude. It does not. Rather, it provides an ideal opportunity to convey a strong message to the buyer about the:

- combined effectiveness of your proposed solution or strategy and business approach
- pride you or your organization have in providing quality service or a product

In other words, why are you or your organization different from the competition?

"Why Us?" Examples

The following example illustrates a "Why Us?" subsection. Note the length and level of detail in this example.

This is an example a data services vendor might use:

Why Federated Computer Systems?

For the last seven years Federated Computer Systems (FCS) has provided unequaled, data processing services to financial institutions. Services unequaled in features, functions, economic value, and quality. Since our beginning, we have based our business on two fundamental operating strategies:

Quality Client Service

When Second Bank of the Southwest (SBS) selects a data processor, it will place its faith and confidence in that organization to deliver quality service — FCS recognizes the critical role its systems and services will play in a SBS' daily operations and ability to effectively and efficiently service SBS customers. Therefore, providing the best quality services available to SBS will always be FCS' primary goal.

Quality at FCS begins with the selection and use of premium data processing hardware and software. However, effective and efficient use of these resources depends on systems, processes, standards, training, and procedures. FCS prides itself on its:

- *conversion programs and procedures*
- *full-time conversion team approach*
- *instructor-led and automated client education programs*
- *on-line and paper-based client documentation*
- *internal employee education programs*
- *on-going resource capacity evaluation and planning programs*
- *full-time Help Desk and toll-free, client support numbers*
- *continuous quality measurements based on the FCS Quality Service Rating System*

Premier Hardware and Software

FCS' only business is to provide data processing services to financial institutions. FCS does not design, develop, or sell hardware or software. FCS firmly believes a data processing service provider faces conflicting goals if it develops, sells, and uses its products.

Rather than limiting hardware or software choices (and services), FCS enjoys the ability to evaluate and select data processing resources from only premier vendors. Further, because of FCS' size, it can strongly influence its vendors' future development plans and enhancements.

"We believe that our activities should be governed by the needs and desires of our customers rather than by our internal requirements and insights."

Eugene F. McCabe
Vice President of Marketing
Merke Sharpe & Dohme
Management, January 1987

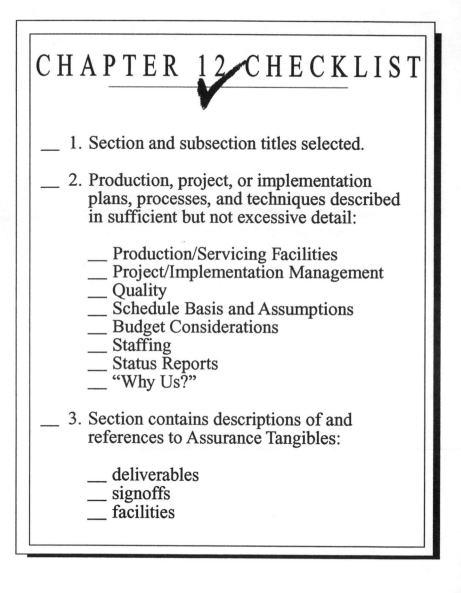

CHAPTER 12 CHECKLIST

__ 1. Section and subsection titles selected.

__ 2. Production, project, or implementation plans, processes, and techniques described in sufficient but not excessive detail:

    __ Production/Servicing Facilities
    __ Project/Implementation Management
    __ Quality
    __ Schedule Basis and Assumptions
    __ Budget Considerations
    __ Staffing
    __ Status Reports
    __ "Why Us?"

__ 3. Section contains descriptions of and references to Assurance Tangibles:

    __ deliverables
    __ signoffs
    __ facilities

CHAPTER 13

◆

SECTION IV: PROJECT OR IMPLEMENTATION PLANS

"Think straight/talk straight."

Arthur Andersen & Co.

Chapter Overview

In this chapter, you will discover why the fourth proposal section holds importance for the proposing individual or organization. You will review the purpose and relevance of this section — a place to define the business-related issues of the proposal, such as schedule, staff, and fees/prices.

You will also review the need to meet two quality dimensions: Reliability and Tangibles. You will then review and examine examples of recommended subsections:

- Assumptions
- Project/Implementation Team
- Project, Implementation, or Production Schedule
- Project/Implementation Fees or Product Prices
- Invoice Schedule

Alternate Section Titles
- Project Plans
- Implementation Plans
- Business Plans

Purpose

This section contains the business issues of your proposed solution or strategy. It should provide the buyer with detailed information on crucial business-related topics such as the proposed:

- project or implementation schedule
- staffing levels
- fees, prices, and project-related expenses
- invoicing schedule
- related fees or expenses

This proposal section must meet two quality dimensions:

Reliability: reflects your ability to identify creative, dependable, and realistic solutions and strategies, and match them to the buyer's needs and wants

Tangibles: enhances and supports the communication of your message and invites readership by its overall appearance, content, and organization

The operative words for these two quality dimensions are realistic, dependable, and communicative. The proposal must communicate these business issues to avoid ambiguity and confusion. In other words, think straight and write straight.

Assumptions

Unless you can see into the future, you must base some of the proposal's business issues on your:

- past experiences with similar production situations, projects, or product implementations
- understanding of the buyer's needs and wants
- estimates on the scope and magnitude of the proposed production, project or product implementation

Disclosing the assumptions used to create the business side of your proposal also answers some questions the buyer may have regarding schedules, fees, etc. The buyer will respect and appreciate the openness demonstrated by revealing your assumptions.

Your proposal should only disclose the major assumptions used to build the business portion of your proposal. Do not include nonessential assumptive detail. Your assumptions should identify and discuss references to:

- production run and time estimates
- assessments of the future market conditions for needed raw materials
- your organization's planned project or implementation staffing levels
- the buyer's specific business operations affected by your proposed solution or strategy
- planned or expected project deliverables
- required involvement or commitment of the buyer's staff or resources
- other variables that can affect timing, scheduling, or pricing

Assumption Examples

The following examples show how you can candidly communicate the assumptions used to formulate the business portion of the proposal.

This is an example of assumptions used by a software and professional services vendor:

> *PreciseSelect, Incorporated (PSI) bases the project's staffing levels, schedule, and estimated fees on the following assumptions:*
>
> - *New Tellers are the target audience for the Automated Employee Selection System – selection tests and computer-aided interviews*
> - *The selection tests will contain 65-70 questions.*
> - *The computer-aided interviews will contain 20 critical incident scenarios*
> - *The project will also develop the following supplementary support materials:*
>   - *Administrator's Guide*
>   - *Interviewer's Manual*
> - *First State Bank of Texas (FSBT) staff will participate on the Project Team with:*
>   - *Human Resources Division and Branch Operations Department staff to assist during the design and testing phases*
>   - *a representative group of Tellers for validity testing*

This is an example of assumptions used by a manufacturer:

> *Towrite Trailers bases their custom boat trailer manufacturing proposal to Sea Sled Boats on the following assumptions:*
>
> - *Towrite will design and manufacture custom trailers for the following Sea Sled models:*
>   - *15' Playmate*
>   - *16' Skimate*
>   - *18' Invader*
>   - *21' Coastal Cruiser*

- *Sea Sled custom trailer production estimates over the three-year contract term:*

BOAT MODEL	1993	1994	1995
15' Playmate	*450*	*600*	*750*
16' Skimate	*525*	*675*	*900*
18' Invader	*450*	*575*	*700*
21' Coastal Cruiser	*250*	*350*	*500*

- *Sea Sled Boats will assign design and engineering staff to assist Towrite in their Custom Trailer Development Process*
- *Towrite estimates their raw material and trailer component costs will rise at an annual average rate of three and one-half percent (3.5%) each year*

Project Team

If your proposed solution or strategy specifies a project team approach, the proposal should define:

- team size
- roles
- responsibilities
- commitment levels

If you know who on your staff will be assigned to the buyer's project, list their names. By identifying project team member assignments, you can turn this subsection of the proposal into a powerful "Assurance Tangible."

Project Team Examples

The following examples illustrate two Project Team subsections. Note the level of detail in each.

Here is an example of a Project Team subsection for a data processing service provider:

Federated Computer Systems (FCS) will assign a dedicated, eight-person Client Conversion Team to Southwest Mutual Savings Bank (SMSB). This team's goal will be to convert SMSB's in-house data processing systems to FCS' Financial Application Systems and services. Each team member will have the following responsibilities for their assigned application systems:

- *conversion program specifications*
- *client processing parameters*
- *pre-conversion testing*
- *pre-conversion client staff training*
- *conversion balancing*
- *post-conversion support (two weeks)*

The following FCS staff will comprise the Client Conversion Team:

FCS STAFF	APPLICATION(S)
Joan Benton	DDA, MMA, and Savings
Bill Winston	CDs and Time Deposits
Sue Alston	IRAs
Steve Wills	Installment Loans
Kathy Mack	Central Information File
Bob Rawlins	Commercial Loans
Janis Coplin	On-line Teller
Dick Mills	Proof of Deposit and Transit

(See Appendix D for biographical data on the Client Conversion Team members.)

The following example illustrates both roles, responsibilities, and commitment levels. Note, this example also includes the expected commitment levels of the buyer's staff on the proposed project.

PreciseSelect, Incorporated (PSI) will assign the following staff from their Professional Services Department to First State Bank of Texas' project:

TITLE	ROLE / RESPONSIBILITIES
Project Manager	• *Primary client contact* • *Project management* • *Selection test design review* • *Computer-aided Interview design review* • *Pilot Test Plan development* • *Implementation Plan develpment* • *Quality control* • *Post-installation review*
Industrial Psychologist	• *Selection test design* • *Computer-aided Interview design* • *Validation and testing* • *Pilot testing*
Analyst	• *Technical design* • *Selection question and computer-aided interview development* • *Test development and testing* • *Validation and testing*

FSBT and PSI will staff phases I through VI of the project as follows (expressed in % commitment level):

ORGANIZATION	POSITION	PHASES					
		I	II	III	IV	V	VI
FSBT	Project Coordinator	25	25	25	25	25	25
	Human Resources	50	50	15	25	25	10
	Branch Automation	50	50	15	25	25	10
PSI	Project Manager	50	25	25	25	25	25
	Industrial Psychologist	100	100	100	50	50	50
	Analyst #1	0	50	100	100	30	50
	Analyst #2	0	50	100	100	30	50

Schedule

Your proposed solution or strategy will impact the buyer's business. Therefore, your production, project, or implementation schedule will directly affect the buyer by determining when a critical project is completed, new product or service is introduced, or a new system is implemented.

Because your proposed solution or strategy will make or save money for the buyer's organization, your schedule becomes very important to acheiving their profitability and productivity goals. Therefore, this subsection must become another "Assurance Tangible" for your buyer. As you will see in the following examples, the Schedule subsection can greatly influence the buyer's perceptions of you or your organization.

Schedule Examples

Your schedule needs to show sufficient and realistic detail to assure the buyer of your ability to perform the work and meet the schedule.

For example, two consultants are proposing to study some aspect of the buyer's operation. One consultant's proposal simply states:

> *"The proposed study will take sixteen (16) working days to complete."*

The other consultant uses basic project management principals in her proposal and includes the following table:

The proposed study activities and estimated timeframes are as follows:

TASK/ ACTIVITY	ESTIMATED DURATION	TOTAL TIME
On-site interviews/information gathering	5 days	5 days
Identify issues & outline study document	2 days	7 days
Review outline with management	1 day	8 days
Draft study document	4 days	12 days
Review draft document with management	1 day	13 days
Finalize study document	3 days	16 days

Which technique helps reduce the buyer's perceived risk or assures the buyer of the consultants abilities? Which consultant has a better chance of getting the engagement?

More on Project Management

Using basic project management techniques can also assure the buyer of your organization's ability to produce, deliver, or implement the product or service.

For example, a company proposing to build and install new signs for a fast food store's 25 locations could use a simple bar chart to reassure the buyer of their ability to deliver.

Acme Sign Company can produce and install the new store signs over a six (6) week period. The following bar chart illustrates our activities and estimated schedule:

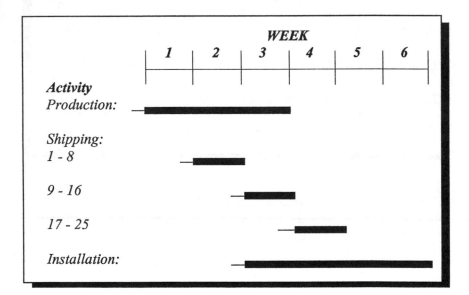

The proposal could also include estimated project or implementation activity start and stop dates. For example, a software and professional services vendor could use their project phases to establish a schedule.

PreciseSelect Incorporated (PSI) understands First State Bank (FSBT) needs to quickly enhance their new Teller selection and interview processes. To accommodate this need, PSI is prepared to begin project activities within 30 days of FSBT's acceptance of this proposal. The following table illustrates our estimated implementation schedule:

PHASE	PHASE NAME/ ACTIVITIES	START	STOP
1	Analysis & Design	04-15	05-13
2	Detail Design • Selection Test Design • Computer-aided Interview (CAI) Design	05-20 05-20 06-06	06-12 06-06 06-12
3	Development • Selection Tests • CAI	06-11 06-11 06-15	07-23 07-02 07-23
4	Testing • Selection Tests • CAI Tests	07-16 07-16 07-25	08-05 07-22 08-05
5	Implementation • AESS (software) • Tests • CAI	07-09 07-09 07-29 08-10	08-26 07-21 08-26 08-26
6	Operation	09-03	

Fees/Prices

The Project Fees subsection of the proposal has great importance to your buyer and you or your organization. This subsection defines how you established your fees and/or prices. This subsection obligates, although normally not legally, you or your organization to deliver the proposed service or product at the fees/prices stated. Therefore, double-check your calculations and get them reviewed and approved by your proposal team.

Several factors can influence this subsection's length and level of detail. These factors include the:

- complexity and length of the project or product implementation
- combination of service fees and product prices
- term of a production contract
- mixture of different product model types, sizes, etc.

This subsection of your proposal also should include other production, project, or implementation costs and expenses such as travel-related expenses, printing or duplication costs, shipping costs, and permit fees.

Fees/Prices Examples

If you or your organization use a project management approach, list your fees by phase. For example, a software and professional services vendor would need to list their software license fee and phased implementation project fees in this proposal subsection:

PSI's fees for the project are:

- *Automated Employee Selection System*
  Permanent License Fee: *$75,000.00*

- *Project Fees:*
  Phase Description

1	*Analysis and Design:*	*$ 5,000.00*	
2	*Detail Design:*	*10,000.00*	
3	*Development:*	*15,000.00*	
4	*Pilot Testing:*	*7,500.00*	
5	*Implementation:*	*7,500.00*	
6	*Operation:*	*5,000.00*	
			50,000.00

- *Travel-related Expenses**   *6,000.00*

  Sales Tax (software only) @6.25%   *4,687.50*

  TOTAL   *$135,687.50*

* *PSI estimates travel-related expenses, which includes air and ground transportation, lodging, and meals, for its staff at $6,000 for the project. PSI will invoice FSBT for these expenses on a monthly basis.*

A manufacturer may need to list product prices over the term of a contract:

Towrite Trailers estimates custom trailer prices for Sea Sled's boats over the three-year contract as follows:

BOAT MODEL	1993*	1994**	1995**
15' Playmate	$1550	$1605	$1660
16' Skimate	$1625	$1682	$1741
18' Invader	$1900	$1967	$2035
21' Coastal Cruiser	$2250	$2329	$2410

* Fixed prices established at the end of Towrite's Custom Trailer Design Process

** Prices based on 1991 estimates with annual raw material and trailer component cost increases estimated at 3.5%.

Note: The above prices are F.O.B. Canton, Texas. Towrite estimates the fees to ship trailers to Sea Sled's plant in Memphis, Tennessee, will add $100-$125 to the price of each trailer.

Invoice Schedule

If you or your organization plans to invoice for the proposed service or product on a non-routine basis, your proposal should define your invoicing schedule. You may also want to include an "Invoice Schedule" subsection if you are working within your buyers budget constraints.

Your invoices would be timed to coincide with the availability of budgeted funds. Further, an invoice schedule will eliminate future questions and ensure timely payment.

Invoice schedules for services projects and product implementations often reflect the completion of a deliverable or major activity or phase. If you or your organization use project management techniques, you can easily tie invoices to phases and milestones.

Invoice Schedule Example

The following example models an "Invoice Schedule" subsection for a software and professional services vendor:

PSI will invoice as follows:

Software Licensee Fee:
- *One-half (1/2) of the total License Fee when PSI receives the accepted AESS License Agreement from First State Bank of Texas*
- *One-half (1/2) of the total License Fee upon project completion*

Project Fees:
- *Phases 1 - 3:*

  One-half (1/2) of each Phase's fee upon initiation of project activities and one-half (1/2) upon completion of the Phase deliverables.

- *Phases 4 - 6:*

  Upon completion of Phase activities and deliverables.

  Travel-related Expenses: At the end of each month

CHAPTER 13 CHECKLIST

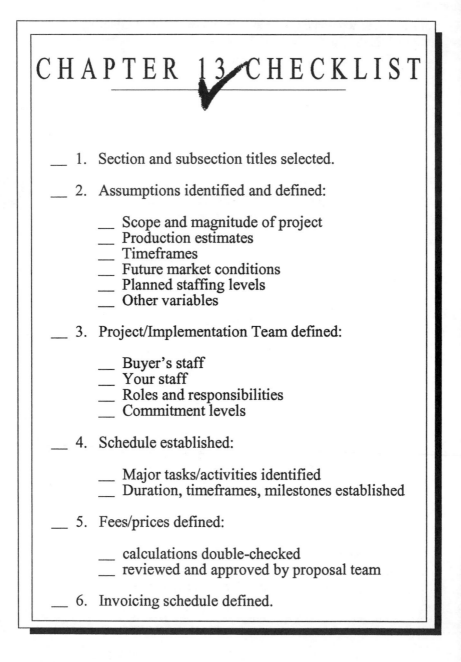

___ 1. Section and subsection titles selected.

___ 2. Assumptions identified and defined:

    ___ Scope and magnitude of project
    ___ Production estimates
    ___ Timeframes
    ___ Future market conditions
    ___ Planned staffing levels
    ___ Other variables

___ 3. Project/Implementation Team defined:

    ___ Buyer's staff
    ___ Your staff
    ___ Roles and responsibilities
    ___ Commitment levels

___ 4. Schedule established:

    ___ Major tasks/activities identified
    ___ Duration, timeframes, milestones established

___ 5. Fees/prices defined:

    ___ calculations double-checked
    ___ reviewed and approved by proposal team

___ 6. Invoicing schedule defined.

CHAPTER 14

APPENDICES: THE PLACE FOR DETAIL

Chapter Overview

By reading this chapter, you will understand the purposes served by appendices:

- to control the length and detail level in the main proposal sections
- a place for preprinted materials

Next you will review guidelines concerning the use of appendices:

- what the buyer expects
- why to maintain the flow
- how to use the proposal team

You will then analyze:

- two rules for using appendices: the dangling appendix rule and order of reference rule
- Appendix versus main section guidelines and examples: how a writer can control the length and detail level of the proposal main section with appendices
- three frequently used appendices:
  - staff biographies
  - client list
  - Gantt or bar chart

Purposes

Proposal appendices serve several useful purposes, they:

* allow the writer to control the detail level and length of the main proposal sections to:
  - maintain reader focus
  - ensure the uninterrupted and systematic flow of logic and ideas
  - avoid overloading and confusing the reader with too much information
* provide a convenient location and method to organize and label:
  - preprinted materials
  - complex charts, tables, and diagrams – product/system/service specifications
  - examples, test results, and lists

Placing preprinted materials in a main proposal section may interrupt the flow and/or ruin a proposal's overall appearance. The proposal writer should answer this question, "Why do I want the reader to read this material?" More than likely, the writer wants the reader to get some information or detail from the material that is not in the proposal. If this is the case, the proposal writer needs to summarize the preprinted material and direct the reader to an appendix for more detail.

Guidelines

Some guidelines to follow when deciding to use appendices include:

Avoid the Expectations/Perceptions Gap. Ask your internal sponsor what his or her organization expects. Some buyers may want proposals that are less than ten pages. Other buyers will want to see all supporting details and information in the main proposal sections.

Maintain the flow. A proposal writer commits a gross error by interrupting the proposal's flow of logic and ideas— interrupting the flow with excessive, unnecessary, and irrelevant details and information. If a piece of information or a detail calculation is not needed to support a point, consider moving it to an appendix.

Use the proposal team. An earlier chapter recommended that the proposal team and writer outline the proposal before writing the first draft. This process should help identify proposal sections that, when written, may be too long. Decide at the outline stage what to put into appendices.

Appendices Rules

Follow these two rules concerning proposal appendices:

Dangling Appendix Rule. Never include an appendix in your proposal that is not referenced in one of the main proposal sections. In other words, leave out an appendix if at least one main proposal section does not contain a reference that directs the reader to that appendix for more information or detail.

Order of Reference Rule. The sequence of appendices should reflect the order in which they are referenced. The first appendix referenced will be A, the next B, etc.

Main Section versus Appendix

The following examples illustrate how easy a writer can control the size of a main proposal section using appendices. In the first example, the writer has decided to move detail from a main section to an appendix.

The main proposal section originally read:

> *First State Bank of Texas' (FSBT's) new Teller selection costs can vary depending upon:*
>
> * *internal cost accounting methods*
> * *labor market conditions*
> * *annual turnover rates and resulting volumes*

Most surveys place the average employment cost for a hourly, clerical employee at $1,500.00. FSBT's Human Resources Division staff stated this cost estimate is very reasonable for their operation. Therefore, FSBT's total annual employment costs for new Tellers hired into metropolitan area Branches are:

- *Total number of new Tellers hired annually:*   *394*
- *Percentage of Tellers hired for metropolitan Branches:*   *80%*
- *Total number of new Tellers that go through the Human Resources Division's selection process (394 x 80%):*   *315*
- *Average employment cost per new Teller:*   *$1,500*

Total Annual Costs (315 x $1,500)   *$472,500*

After moving most of the detail to an appendix, the section would read:

First State Bank of Texas' (FSBT's) new Teller selection costs can vary depending upon:

- *internal cost accounting methods*
- *labor market conditions*
- *annual turnover rates and resulting volumes*

FSBT's total employment costs for the 315 new Tellers hired into metropolitan area Branches each year are $472,500. See Appendix B for more detail.

In the second example, a proposal contains the following table:

PHASE	PHASE NAME/ ACTIVITIES	START	STOP
1	Analysis & Design	04-15	05-13
2	Detail Design • Selection Test Design • CAI Design	05-20 05-20 06-06	06-12 06-06 06-12
3	Development • Selection Tests • CAI	06-11 06-11 06-15	07-23 07-02 07-23
4	Testing • Selection Tests • CAI	07-16 07-16 07-25	08-05 07-22 08-05
5	Implementation • AESS (software) • Tests • CAI	07-09 07-09 07-29 08-10	08-26 07-21 08-26 08-26
6	Operation	09-03	

If the writer's proposal team thought that the above table contained too much detail, the writer could summarize the information:

PHASE	PHASE NAME/ ACTIVITIES	START	STOP
1	Analysis & Design	04-15	05-13
2	Detail Design	05-20	06-12
3	Development	06-11	07-23
4	Testing	07-16	08-05
5	Implementation	07-09	08-26
6	Operation	09-03	

(See Appendix F for a more detailed project schedule.)

Or, the writer could summarize the entire table and reference an appendix:

We can start the project on April 15, and estimate the system will be operational the beginning of September. See Appendix F for a more detailed project schedule.

The Biographical Resume Appendix

For most service proposals, the expertise of the proposed project staff may become a deciding factor for vendor selection. In these cases, your proposal must contain a brief biographical resume for each proposed project team member. Individual resumes should include the following information:

- position held within the organization
- professional experience as it applies or relates to the project
- educational background and trade association affiliations

Biographical Resume Example

The following example illustrates a bio that a software and professional services vendor might use in a proposal appendix.

Appendix C

Knowledge Systems Incorporated
Staff Bios

Mark W. Kincaid

Mr. Kincaid is a Senior Director at Knowledge Systems, Inc. (KSI). At KSI, Mark is responsible for client/project administration and new business development. Mark has managed the client relations and development projects for 2nd Florida Bank, 1st Stateside Bank, and American Motor Car Company. Mark joined KSI after selling his company, Computer Learning Systems (CLS), to KSI in 1989.

Prior to founding CLS in 1985, Mark was Vice President and Manager of WTech's, CBT business unit and was responsible for identifying and developing CBT courseware as a new product line. Prior to his involvement with CBT, Mark was in charge of product development and management for WTech's commercial banking application systems.

Before joining WTech, Mark held positions with two large commercial banks: Project Manager, Manager of an Electronic Banking Systems department, and various positions in marketing, product development, and customer service in a data processing department.

Mr. Kincaid has a B.B.A. from Michigan State University and several American Institute of Banking Certificates. Mark has been a frequent speaker at various regional and national automated education conventions including: The CBI Conference, CBLE-SW, and ASLD.

The Client List Appendix

The Client List appendix serves three important purposes:

* identify past and present clients
* provide a contact for the buyer to call for a reference
* emphasize your organization's customer-driven nature

Optionally, this appendix can include a brief description of the product, product implementation, project, or other appropriate information for each client listed.

Client Reference Rules

Follow these simple rules before listing any of your clients:

* ask permission to use them as a reference to insure it does not violate their policies or will not make the client contact feel uncomfortable
* double-check names, titles, and phone numbers
* question and coach the client contact to insure his or her organization:
  - received value for their money—your services or products met the client's expectations ("walked the talk")
  - felt you or your organization handled the project or product implementation in a professional and quality manner
  - will confirm that you or your organization have the ability and resources to perform the project

Client List Examples

The following examples illustrate two Client List appendix formats:

Appendix F
Client References

XYZ Manufacturing Company
123 Corporate Drive
Phoenix, Arizona 85221

Client Contact: **Ms. Susan A. Young,**
Senior Engineer
602-555-3746

Philman Fabricating
8594 W. Congress Avenue
Peoria, Illinois 37245

Client Contact: **Mr. John S. Philman,**
President
312-555-5828

OR

Appendix F
Client References

CLIENT REFERENCE	CONTACT
XYZ Manuafacturing Company *123 Corporate Drive* *Phoenix, Arizona 85221*	**Ms. Susan A. Young,** *Senior Engineer* *602-555-3746*
Philman Fabricating *8594 W. Congress Avvenue* *Peoria, Illinois 37245*	**Mr. John S. Philman,** *President* *312-555-5828*

Gantt or Bar Chart Appendix

If your proposed solution or strategy involves a complex and lengthy project or implementation, you should consider using a Gantt or bar chart to illustrate your estimated schedule. This provides the buyer with another Assurance Tangible which:

- indicates you have completed preliminary planning
- reflects your approach to the project or implementation
- provides estimated project dates, timeframes and milestones

Here are some guidelines for these charts:

- list only major tasks/activities
- use a realistic timeline scale:
  - a two to four month project might use a weekly timeline
  - a four month or longer project might use a monthly timeline
- limit the Gantt or bar chart to one or two pages (unless the proposed solution or strategy requires a very complex or lengthy project/ implementation)

Gantt/Bar Chart Example

The following Gantt or bar chart example illustrates a reasonable level of detail and proper timeline for the proposed project.

Appendix G

XYZ Manufacturing
Estimated Project Schedule

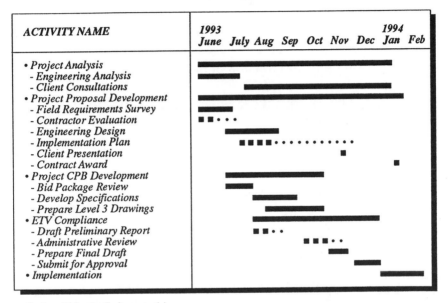

ACTIVITY NAME	1993 June July Aug Sep Oct Nov Dec 1994 Jan Feb
• Project Analysis	
- Engineering Analysis	
- Client Consultations	
• Project Proposal Development	
- Field Requirements Survey	
- Contractor Evaluation	
- Engineering Design	
- Implementation Plan	
- Client Presentation	
- Contract Award	
• Project CPB Development	
- Bid Package Review	
- Develop Specifications	
- Prepare Level 3 Drawings	
• ETV Compliance	
- Draft Preliminary Report	
- Administrative Review	
- Prepare Final Draft	
- Submit for Approval	
• Implementation	

Scale: 1 Month=5 character(s)
Normal: ▬▬▬▬
Critical: ■ ■ ■
Slack: • • •

CHAPTER 14 CHECKLIST

___ 1. Appendices titles selected.

___ 2. Use of appendices reviewed and approved by the:

    ___ buyer

    ___ proposal team

___ 3. No dangling appendices.

___ 4. Appendices in order of reference.

CHAPTER 15

◆

QUALITY PRODUCTION AND DELIVERY: PUTTING IT ALL TOGETHER

"Quality is very simple. So simple, in fact, that it is difficult for people to understand it."

Roger Hale
CEO, Tennant Co.
Quest for Quality (Tennant, 1987)

Chapter Overview

In this chapter, you will briefly review the benefits and capabilities of word processing and desktop publishing software. You will then examine some proposal production guidelines: quality, time and expense, overuse/ abuse of technology, and content versus form.

Next you will study:

- the proposal's Cover Page and Table of Contents plus examples of each
- several proposal production issues, such as: page numbering, printing and binding, number of copies, etc.
- the Letter of Transmittal: purpose, contents, and an example
- proposal delivery and the possible need to coach the internal sponsor if he or she will present the proposal to the buyer's organization

Word Processing & Desktop Publishing

Personal computers enable even the smallest company to produce documents with a professional appearance. Word processing software provides the ability to simultaneously write and edit, automatically number pages, check a document's spelling and grammar, embed graphics and charts. Desktop publishing software offers advanced graphical capabilities and typeset print quality. With these tremendous production capabilities, everyone has the ability to produce a proposal with "drive-up appeal."

Some Production Guidelines

With all the available technology, the question becomes, is the sales proposal a work of art or a business document? To some degree, it is a balanced combination. When producing a proposal, the selling organization should use all the production resources available, physically and financially, within the following guidelines:

Quality. Remember, the proposal becomes the first tangible deliverable for the buyer [future customer]. Above all, it should represent the highest possible quality. This book's *Quality Proposal RATER* specifically identifies the proposal's overall appearance under the Tangible dimension.

Time & Expense. The expense to develop a proposal is significant, it includes: the salesperson's and proposal team's time and any travel-related expenses associated with the sales calls. The selling organization needs to consider the additional time and expense associated with elaborate proposal production techniques. The proposing organization should answer these questions:

- What are the buyer's expectations?
- Will an elaborate proposal make a difference or will it overshadow the proposal's message?
- What do we have to do to differentiate our proposal from that of the competition?

Overuse/Abuse of Technology. The most important component of a proposal is its content. An organization can demonstrate an overuse or abuse of technology in their proposals if page headers and footers obscure the content of the pages themselves or graphics confuse rather than clarify — distract rather than attract the reader.

Content Versus Form. A sales proposal should be an artfully produced business document. Unless the organization is trying to sell desktop publishing or graphics software, laser printers, or color plotters, the proposal's form should never dominate its content. A proposal should impress the reader with the quality of its message, not the complex techniques used to produce the proposal itself.

However, a proposal's form should reflect the ever-increasing expectations in today's marketplace. If a major competitor uses desktop publishing to produce its proposals, then a competing proposal must match or exceed the competition.

Cover Page

All proposals need a cover page containing four components, the:

- buyer's name
- name of the proposal
- date of the proposal
- name of your organization or your name

Optionally, the cover page can include the buyer's *or* your organization's logo.

The following page illustrates a sample proposal cover page:

Exhibit 15.1

FIRST STATE BANK OF TEXAS

A Proposal to Implement

an

Automated Employee Selection System

July 4, 1993

PreciseSelect, Incorporated
Austin, Texas

Table of Contents

The Table of Contents appears at the front of the proposal. It serves two useful purposes; it provides a quick view of the proposal's entire contents, and saves time when a reader wants to look up a particular item.

The table of contents should list:

* sections
* subsections
* appendices
* illustrations
* page numbers

Table of Contents Example

The following exhibit illustrates the format of a Table of Contents:

Exhibit 15.2

TABLE OF CONTENTS

Page i

Page Numbers

Number all proposal pages, except the cover or title page. Follow these guidelines:

Table of Contents and Executive Summary. Use non-capitalized Roman numerals (i, ii, iii, etc.) as page numbers.

Main Proposal Sections. Use consecutive page numbers for all main proposal section pages, including pages containing charts, graphics, tables, etc. The first page of the first main section is page 1.

Appendices. Use each appendix's alphabetical designation as part of its page number. For example, if Appendix B is three pages long, its page numbers would be B-1, B-2, and B-3.

Printing & Binding

How a proposal has been printed and bound will strongly influence the proposal readers' first impression of your organization's concern for quality. It also shows how much you value the buyer or their potential business.

Do not make a costly mistake by scrimping on the proposal's paper, cover, or binding. For a few dollars your proposal can have a quality, professional appearance. Conversely, unless the buyer expects to receive a leather-bound proposal, do not become too extravagant.

Printers. We recommend using a laser printer. However, if you are using a NLR (near letter quality) dot-matrix printer:

- use a new ribbon to print the final proposal;
- then use this final proposal as the master for making copies, most copy machines will improve the appearance of a dot-matrix printer's output.

Paper Weight. Do not print or copy the final proposal on the standard 20# paper used in most copiers or printers. For pennies more, you can use a heavier-weight, bonded paper for your proposal.

Binding. Never send your buyer a proposal that is *only* stapled together. This sends a negative message — no quality, stability, or permanence. Go to a printer for help – most printers can offer several options at very reasonable prices. Make this investment, it will pay off.

Some Tips & Ideas

Preprinted Covers. If you can afford preprinted proposal covers, buy them. For $150-$350, you can significantly enhance the appearance of your next 100+ proposals. Preprinted covers send two very strong messages; a concern for projecting a quality image, and stability or permanence.

Section Indexes/Dividers. Preprinted section dividers are perhaps the ultimate technique for establishing proposal "drive-up appeal." Combined with a preprinted cover, a proposal with preprinted section dividers looks good even before the reader opens to the first page. One word of caution: make sure that when closed, the proposal's cover conceals the dividers. Protruding dividers will distract from the overall appearance.

Never use inexpensive blank dividers and a typewriter to make do-it-yourself proposal dividers. This technique cheapens the appearance.

Number of Copies. Ask your internal sponsor or champion how many proposal copies are needed. If a committee or team will review the proposal, make sure each member gets an original. Never let a decision-maker review an internally copied version of your proposal.

Letter of Transmittal

Use the Letter of Transmittal as the cover letter for sending your proposal to the buyer. Writing this letter demonstrates proper business etiquette.

The Letter of Transmittal should:

- confirm why the proposal is being submitted, e.g., a request from the buyer, response to an RFP (Request for Proposal), etc.
- briefly mention the buyer's needs and wants and your proposed solution's major benefits
- highlight your "Why Us?" section
- offer to provide additional information, in any form, if requested or needed by the buyer:
  - telephone conversation
  - informal meeting
  - formal presentation
- acknowledge the time and support of the buyer and his or her staff in assisting you to complete the proposal

Address the Letter of Transmittal to your internal sponsor or whomever requested the proposal. The Letter of Transmittal should be no more than two pages long.

Most organizations bind a copy of the Letter of Transmittal behind the cover page of each proposal— this gives all proposal readers an opportunity to read it.

Letter of Transmittal Example
The following example illustrates a typical Letter of Transmittal.

Exhibit 15.3

PreciseSelect, Incorporated
1275 North Conway Blvd
Austin, Texas 75012

June 4, 1993

Ms. Doris Quinlin,
Senior Vice President
First State Bank of Texas
1 FSBT Center
Dallas, Texas 75201

Dear Ms. Quinlin:

PreciseSelect, Incorporated (PSI) appreciates the opportunity to submit the enclosed proposal for your review and consideration. We have prepared this proposal in response to your request to present proven methods for reducing First State Bank of Texas' high Teller turnover rate. This high Teller turnover rate has resulted in:

* *escalating selection, hiring, and training expenses*
* *lower customer service levels at the Bank's branches*

PSI's industrial psychologists have conducted numerous studies and research projects to determine the causes for employee turnover. Their findings overwhelming pointed to one primary cause — ineffective and inconsistent employee selection and hiring techniques. PSI's Automated Employee and Selection System (AESS) offers a proven solution by using:

- *unbiased and validated computer-based selection tests to pre-screen applicants*
- *computer-based interviews to evaluate applicant responses to critical incident situations*

Over the past eight years, PSI has implemented AESS in over 100 major corporations. All of these clients realized a payback on their investment in the first six to nine months. These clients continue to use PSI's annual evaluation services to update and re-validate their tests and interview scenarios.

As we agreed, I will present AESS and this proposal to your Bank's Senior Management Committee meeting on June 18 at 9:00 a.m. If you have any questions before the meeting, please call me at 1-800-555-TEST.

Thank you again for giving PSI this opportunity. Personally, I would also like to thank you and your staff for taking time from your busy schedules to help me gather the information needed to develop this proposal. I look forward to working with you and your staff in the future.

Sincerely,

Bart L. Roberts
Regional Manager

enclosure

BLR:mf

Delivery

Physically delivering the proposal does not mean that you have completed your selling assignment. Rather, the buyer's next step may dictate further action.

* If your sponsor does not have the authority to sign the contract, you may have to coach him or her on how to sell your service or product into the organization.
* If your sponsor plans to present your proposal to senior management or a committee, you may have to coach him or her on how to use the proposal for this purpose.
* If your sponsor is not comfortable presenting the proposal, he or she may ask you to present the proposal to senior management or a committee.

Whatever the situation, having delivered a quality proposal to the buyer certainly puts you and your organization in an advantageous position. A quality proposal lowers risk of failure and greatly improves chances for success.

Coaching the Internal Sponsor

If your internal sponsor plans to present your proposal, you may want or need to give him or her some coaching to help insure your success. Coaching, not from the standpoint of how to present, but coaching on what to present. If you have worked closely with the internal sponsor throughout the sales process, he or she should need little help with understanding and presenting the proposal's content. However, you may want to review the following proposal presentation guidelines with your sponsor:

Use the proposal to guide the presentation. Suggest your sponsor follow the proposal's organization in the presentation. This offers several advantages, as it:

* provides the most logical approach for reviewing the entire proposal
* insures that the sponsor follows the proposal's systematic discovery of needs/wants and presentation of solutions or strategies
* helps keep the audience on track, especially those who have not read the proposal in advance

Highlight key points from each proposal section. Prepare your sponsor for the presentation the same way you would prepare yourself. Suggest he or she either list or highlight or underline the key points within each section. Recommend he or she cover each of these key points during the presentation. Insure that your sponsor particularly emphasizes:

* his or her organization's current revenues or costs, needs and wants
* how the proposed solution satisfies those needs and wants: non-financial [qualitative] benefits and financial [quantitative] benefits – "walk the talk"
* how your organization does business, plans to approach this project or implementation, and why you or your organization satisfy the buyer's criteria for value, quality, and price

Obtain an agreement. Make sure your internal sponsor understands that his or her primary goal is to secure approval on your proposal and get a signed contract.

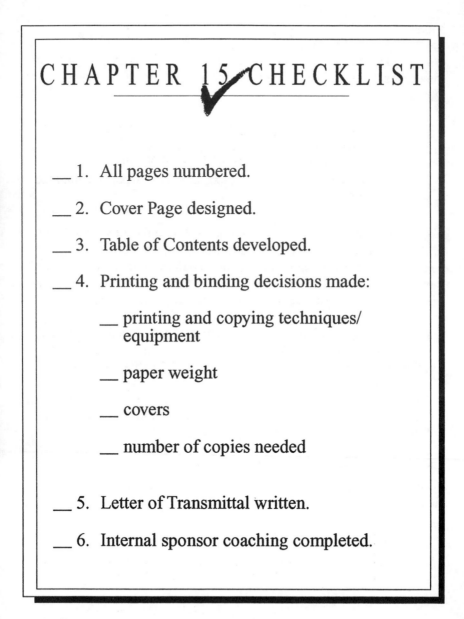

CHAPTER 15 CHECKLIST

___ 1. All pages numbered.

___ 2. Cover Page designed.

___ 3. Table of Contents developed.

___ 4. Printing and binding decisions made:

    ___ printing and copying techniques/
    equipment

    ___ paper weight

    ___ covers

    ___ number of copies needed

___ 5. Letter of Transmittal written.

___ 6. Internal sponsor coaching completed.

CHAPTER 16

$\blacklozenge$

THE RECOMMENDATION REPORT:
AN INTERNAL SALES PROPOSAL

---

*"Forced to choose among irrelevant alternatives on the
basis of misleading facts, and without the benefit of solid
analysis, even the best judgement can do little but grope
intuitively in the dark."*

Charles L. Schultze
Director, U.S. Bureau of Budget
Senate testimony, August 23, 1967

Chapter Overview

In this chapter, you will:

- learn about internal selling—how to sell solutions to internal problems or opportunities
- be presented with a six-step internal sales system
- review the Position Paper, a document used to initiate a study and to secure team resources for analyzing an internal problem or opportunity
- review the Recommendation Report — the *internal sales proposal*, the report used to document the study team's analyzes, conclusions, and recommendations

Selling Internally

Writing quality internal sales proposals or Recommendation Reports can be as critical to a company's success as a writing winning sales proposals. Often times one person or a team within an organization identifies a problem or opportunity that can make or save money (or improve productivity or profitability). If the problem or opportunity is complex, costly to implement, or crosses organizational lines, selling the idea maybe difficult. Further, the idea may require an in-depth analysis of several alternatives and the expertise of a cross-functional team.

Most individuals face several dilemmas when confronted with this situation. They do not know:

- how to internally sell a new idea or concept
- how to thoroughly evaluate and document viable alternatives, draw conclusions, and make recommendations
- what to include in a report for review by senior management, a task force, or strategic planning group
- how to structure a report, that if approved, provides all the needed commitments for implementing the recommended change

The Recommendation Report, as an internal sales proposal, can provide an effective means for selling within an organization.

Informal and Formal Processes

In some organizations, writing a Recommendation Report may be the result of an informal process. An individual may not need to get management approval prior to analyzing a problem or opportunity. In these situations, one person can informally consult with others in the organization during the analysis and write a report.

Other organizations use a more formal process to complete internal analyses or studies and write Recommendation Reports. In these organizations, management first must approve the commitment of study resources, usually with a "Position Paper." Often a formal study team is formed to analyze the situation and write a report to senior management.

This chapter presents a formal process for writing internal sales proposals or Recommendation Reports. However, the report's format, content, and structure guidelines apply to either a formal or informal analysis process.

An Internal Sales System

If selling activities and writing a sales proposal are processes within a sales system, then, analyzing an internal problem or opportunity and writing a Recommendation Report are processes within an internal sales system. Although the internal sales system may not be as well defined or even named, it does provide a means or method to initiate change within an organization.

Most methodologies have defined steps or phases. Some recommended steps to follow when writing a Recommendation Report include:

Step #1: Identify the Problem or Opportunity

One or more internal staff members may recognize a problem situation or an opportunity to do something different. It may mean changing customer service policies and procedures, implementing a new product line, or replacing one-page quote sheets with customer-driven sales proposals. Whatever the problem or opportunity, these staff members are usually highly motivated. They think they have an idea that will save or make money for the organization. They want to make a difference.

Some questions to ask during Step #1 activities may include:

- What is motivating the proposed study, the need to:
  - save or make money?
  - fix a problem?
  - invest in staff retraining?
  - improve productivity?

- Who is the internal customer?
- What are the political ramifications and who might resent the potential change?
- Have funds been budgeted for a change?
- What is the timeframe for and urgency of change?
- What barriers exist that may impair the project?
- Who or what key functions might contribute to the success of the change?

After diagnosing the problem or opportunity, the idea needs to be documented. An individual or a team member needs to write a memo to a manager, *the internal customer*:

- whose unit will be most affected by the potential change, or
- who requested a preliminary analysis of the problem or opportunity

The memo should be one or two pages long and include the following:

- *Background Information:* An overview of the current situation. This section should include a brief discussion of the problem or opportunity including current costs, revenues, production statistics, etc.
- *Potential Solution (or Strategy):* A brief explanation of how the problem could be solved or how the organization could capitalize on the opportunity. This section should also include a brief discussion of available alternatives and estimated implementation costs, resources, and timeframes.
- *Benefits:* Describe how implementing the solution or strategy will benefit the organization. Provide estimated financial and non-financial benefits.

Send the memo to the internal customer and request a meeting to discuss it.

Step #2: Review with a Manager *(or Internal Customer)*

In most organizations, it is inappropriate not to follow the chain of command. Therefore, as stated in Step #1, an immediate manager should receive the memo and review the idea. In most situations, a manager may add valuable insight into the problem or opportunity. This insight might include such things as, past attempts to correct the problem, reasons why the organization has chosen not to get involved in a certain line of business, etc. The manager also may help with the next step, writing the Position Paper.

Your manager or the internal customer may decide your idea is not viable. He or she may not support advancing it within the organization. If this happens, there are few options:

- perhaps another team member may try to gain support from his or her manager
- further analyze the situation and resubmit the idea at a later date

Step #3: Write the Position Paper

The Position Paper is a *Pre-Recommedation Report*. It can be written in memo format. See "The Position Paper" section of this chapter for structure and contents guidelines.

One key point to keep in mind when writing a Position Paper: The Position Paper lists study team members by name and commitment level; make sure these resources have been secured.

Step #4: Position Paper Approval

Send the Position Paper to the appropriate individual, usually a senior manager or a designated Steering Committee Chairperson, for review and approval. It may be necessary to schedule a review meeting with this individual to answer questions and discuss study strategies. More than likely, this individual will want to review the Position Paper with other senior managers or Steering Committee members before approving the study.

When the individual to whom the Position Paper was sent approves it, the study phase officially begins:

* committed resources are authorized to participate in the study; the Study Team is officially formed
* a Steering Committee is officially formed
* any expenses needed to complete the study are approved

Step #5: Form the Study Team, Analyze the Situation, and Write the Recommendation Report

Upon approval of the Position Paper, the Study Team Leader or Project Manager should advise the appropriate individuals that the Position Paper has been approved and schedule the first Study Team meeting.

Send a copy of this memo to the Steering Committee members.
The activities of the Study Team when analyzing the situation and writing the Recommendation Report closely parallel the activities used to write a sales proposal. The study quickly comes into focus if the Study Team views the Steering Committee Chairperson as their internal customer or buyer. Use the eight proposal writing steps discussed in Chapter 9, *Team Writing the Proposal: Recommended Steps,* to guide the analysis and writing activities. This will help to:

* define Study Team member roles and responsibilities
* establish study goals, activities, and timeframes
* receive preliminary approvals by reviewing the Recommendation Report outline, drafts, and final version with the Steering Committee Chairperson, the internal customer or buyer

Step #6: Steering Committee Review and Approval

Viewing the Steering Committee as an internal buying committee will clarify the Recommendation Report's review and approval process. When the Steering Committee Chairperson approves the final version of the Recommendation Report, he or she should:

- send copies of the report to all the Steering Committee members
- schedule a Steering Committee meeting

At the meeting, the Steering Committee Chairperson or the Study Team Leader will present the Recommendation Report to the Steering Committee members. This meeting will provide the members with an opportunity to ask questions and discuss the findings of the study and the Study Team's recommendations. If the Steering Committee approves (buys) the report, the project or purchase is authorized.

The Position Paper

Although one person can write a Recommendation Report, it is often more effective to use a team approach. Analyzing the problem or opportunity may require the expertise of individuals from different functional areas within the organization. Writing a Position Paper also will solidify support within the organization because it requires the commitment of the team members' time and resources to complete the study and write a Recommendation Report.

Treat the Position Paper as a *"Pre-Recommendation Report."* It should be no more than three or four pages long and written in memo format.

To: Direct the Position Paper to the senior manager whose function will be most affected by the proposed change.

The Position Paper should contain the following sections:

Background Information: A brief discussion of the current situation and the problem or opportunity. Include current:

- revenue, profit, and/or costs
- production or productivity levels statistics
- staffing levels

This section should follow the content guidelines discussed in Chapter 10, *Section I: The Buyer's Business.*

Potential Solution (or Strategy): A overview description of potential solutions or strategies that the proposed study would evaluate, including:

- non-financial and estimated financial benefits that would result if the solution or strategy would be implemented
- estimate implementation resources, costs, and timeframes

Study Resources Required: A detailed listing of the committed study team members, costs, and estimated timeframes needed to analyze the situation and write a Recommendation Report. This section should include:

- required study team members—name and commitment level. *Note: List only the names and commitment levels of study team members who have been secured to participate in the study. Listing study team members whose commitments have not been secured may result in political problems or an aborted study effort.*
- estimated out-of-pocket expenses for fact-finding trips, outside consultants, etc.
- estimated study timeframe

Steering Committee: Identify who will be on the study's Steering Committee and who will be its Chairperson. Ideally, Steering Committee members, including the Chairperson, should be peers within the organization. This will help avoid a situation where one committee member could attempt to dictate the final outcome of the study.

Note: In most situations, the Steering Committee Chairperson should be from the department or division that will be most affected by the change.

Position Paper Example

Memorandum

To:	*Judith A. Harrington, Chief Financial Officer*
From:	*Randolph H. Jones, Senior Auditor*
Date:	*June 14, 1993*
Subject:	*POSITION PAPER - Inventory Control System*

Background Information
The inventory control system currently in use was purchased from ICP in 1979. In 1987, ICP stopped supporting the system when they introduced a new product using advanced data base facilities. Acme's MIS staff have made extensive changes to the system since 1987 including access to the Local Area Network. The MIS Department budgeted $135,000 to support the inventory control system in 1993.

Since 1989, Acme's growth and the resulting changes to its inventory have strained the functional capabilities of the inventory control system. Some significant changes include:

* *an increase in the number of inventory items from 2,100 to 3,350*
* *inventory turnover increased from 6.9 to 11.2 times per year*

*The increased inventory activity coupled with the functional limita-
tions of the data base design of the inventory control system cause
operational problems. Acme is experiencing interface problems
between the inventory control system and the purchasing and
accounts payable systems. These problems result in the need to
manually enter data from certain complex transactions. Three (3)
full-time clerks are required to re-enter these transactions at an
annual cost of $60,000.*

A recent audit, found two major problems:

* *inaccurately priced inventory items*
* *inaccurate inventory levels resulting from lost or erroneous
  purchasing or accounts payable entries*

Potential Solutions

*Based on discussions with the Purchasing, MIS, Inventory and
Accounts Payable managers, Acme has several possible solutions
available:*

* *Use Acme's MIS staff to design and develop a new inventory
  control system at an estimated costs of $250,000; estimated
  project timeframe is ten (10) to fourteen (14) months.*
* *Evaluate commercially-available inventory control systems to
  replace the existing system; estimated licensee fees should range
  from $80,000 to $175,000. An implementation project could cost
  an estimated $100,000 and take from four (4) to six (6) months.*

Study Resources Required
*To complete a comprehensive study of this problem, a Study Team
comprised of the following Acme staff is required:*

Name	Department	Commitment
James Ronson*	Inventory	30%
Barbara Madsen	MIS	30%
Judith Tewes	Purchasing	20%
Rick Sanders	Auditing	20%
Bill Winslow	Plant Operations	20%
Bob Kincaid	Accounts Payable	20%

* Study Team Leader.

The Study Team will need eight (8) weeks to complete its analysis and write a Recommendation Report.

Steering Committee
A Steering Committee is needed to counsel the Study Team and review the Recommendation Report. The following members are requested:

Name	Division
Judith Harrington, SVP/CFO*	Finance
Bill Margold, SVP	Operating Services
G. Gordon Berry, SVP	Manufacturing
Nancy Newell, SVP	MIS

* Steering Committee Chairperson

Recommendation Report

The structure and format of a Recommendation Report should parallel that of a sales proposal. However, there are two sections that will differ in name and content:

Section	in a *Sales Proposal...*	in a *Recommendation Report...*
II	Proposed Solution	Available Solution or Alternative Solutions
III	Implementation or Project Methodology	Conclusions and Recommendations

Therefore, a quality Recommendation Report would include four major sections:

* *Background Information:* describes the current situation and identifies the problem or opportunity facing the organization.
* *Available Solution (or Alternative Solutions):* describes the proposed solution or alternative solutions including costs and non-financial benefits. If the study team has analyzed several alternatives, the report should discuss advantages and disadvantages of each alternative.
* *Conclusions and Recommendations:* reached by the study team. This section also includes the financial or quantitative benefits that the organization would realize by implementing the recommended solution.
* *Project or Implementation Plans:* lists implementation costs, staffing commitments, timeframes, and capital expenditures required to implement the recommended solution (see Chapter 13, *Section IV: Project or Implementation Plans* for detailed information).

Like a quality sales proposal, a Recommendation Report must also contain:

* a *Table of Contents* (see Chapter 15, *Quality Production and Delivery: Putting It All Together* for detailed information)
* an *Executive Summary* (see Chapter 8, *A Quality Proposal: Recommended Structure,* for detailed information)

- if necessary, *Appendices* for supporting information (see Chapter 14, *Appendices: The Place for Detail* for detailed information)

A Recommendation Report should contain all the information needed for senior management to make a *buy* decision.

Section I: Background Information

See Chapter 10, *Section I: The Buyer's Business* for detailed information.

Section II: Available Solution (or Alternative Solutions)

The second Recommendation Report section provides the place to discuss the available solution or alternative solutions to the problem (or opportunity).

If the report presents only one solution, then this section should follow a format similar to that discussed in Chapter 11, *Section II: Your Proposed Solution*. This section would include the following subsections:

Description
- a detailed discussion of the available solution and what it will do or how it will work for the organization
- include functions, features, and specifications

Non-financial or Qualitative Benefits
- a discussion of the value-added aspects of the available solution
- these benefits should specifically relate to the organization (see Chapter 11, *Section II: Your Proposed Solution - Non-financial Benefits Overview* for more information and examples)

Cost
- the estimated cost to implement the solution

In some situations, the study may evaluate several alternative solutions. Include a *Description, Non-financial benefits,* and *Cost* subsection for each alternative as described above.

When discussing each alternative solution include two additional subsections: *Advantages* and *Disadvantages*. These two subsections should reflect the in-depth evaluation done of all the alternatives during the study. These subsections should provide a contrast and compare each alternative to the other alternatives.

Advantages
- the advantages the organization would realize by implementing this alternative instead of the other alternatives

Disadvantages
- the disadvantage the organization would experience if it implemented this alternative instead of the other alternatives

Advantages and Disadvantages Example

The following example illustrates how a Study Team from Acme Manufacturing might describe the advantages and disadvantages for buying or internally developing a new inventory control application software system.

Alternative #1: Buy the Automated Inventory Control System (AICS) from Universal Software Inc.

Description:
Non-financial [quantitative] Benefits:

Costs:

The Advantages for buying AICS are:

- *The system has an installed user base of 68.*
- *Universal Software provides annual software releases and implementation and telephone support.*
- *Acme Manufacturing would not need to contract or hire systems development resources to internally develop a system.*
- *Implementation is estimated at four (4) months.*

- *Over a seven-year useful life analysis, buying AICS is less expensive than building a system internally.*

The Disadvantages for buying AICS are:

- *Purchase of AICS will require a capital expenditure of $150,000.*
- *After the first year, Acme would incur a $22,500 annual AICS maintenance fee to receive the annual releases and ongoing support.*
- *AICS will receive some modification to meet several specialized inter-divisional reporting requirements.*

Alternative #2: Internally develop a new inventory control system.

Description:
Non-financial [quantitative] Benefits

Costs:

The Advantages for internally developing a new inventory control system are:

- *Internal development will not require a capital expenditure of $150,000 for software acquisition*
- *There are no ongoing annual software maintenance expenses of $22,500, estimated at $135,000 over the system's seven year useful life.*
- *Acme's MIS staff can design the system to meet specialized inter-divisional reporting requirements.*

The Disadvantages for internally developing a new inventory control system are:

- *ACME's MIS staff would have to develop the new system at an estimated soft-dollar cost of $235,000.*
- *ACME's MIS staff would have to maintain the system including the development of enhancements.*

- *ACME would need to contract or hire one Systems Analyst and one Programmer to meet the proposed ten (10) month development schedule; estimated cost of $110,000.*
- *Development and implementation are estimated at twelve (12) months.*

Section III: Conclusions and Recommendations

This Recommendation Report section reflects the Study Team's agreement on how to solve the problem or capitalize on the opportunity. It should contain the following subsections:

Conclusions
An overview discussing the Study Team's analysis and agreement on:

- the conditions causing the problem or presenting the opportunity
- the viability of the solution or each alternative solution

Recommendations:
A statement or statements that reflect the Study Team's agreement on:

- the best way to correct the problem or capitalize on the opportunity, the team's recommended solution
- the specific resources, capital expenditures, timeframes, marketing expenses, etc., needed to implement the team's recommendations

Financial or Quantitative Benefits (of the recommended solution)
This is the "Walk the Talk" section of the internal sales proposal. It must present:

- the financial viability of the recommended solution—how it will save or make money for the organization
- financial benefits in terms senior management uses to make financial decisions, for example, estimated earnings, return on investment, years to payback, or increased earnings per share

If a representative from accounting is on your Study Team, assign him or her this subsection. (see Chapter 11, *Section II: Your Proposed Solution - Financial Benefits Overview* for more information and examples).

Conclusions and Recommendations Example

The following example illustrates how a Study Team from Acme Manufacturing might describe their conclusions and recommendations after analyzing the need to implement a new inventory control system.

Conclusions and Recommendations

After analyzing the operation of Acme Manufacturing's present inventory control system, the Study Team has reached the following conclusions and recommendations:

The Study Team concludes the present inventory control system:
1. *Does not provide for the efficient flow of information between the purchasing and accounts payable systems. As a result three (3) full-time clerical positions are needed to resolve input problems and correct receiving and billing errors. The fully loaded annual cost for these three positions is $60,000.*
2. *Uses outmoded data processing data handling techniques and communications protocols. The current system is based on a system purchased from ICP in 1979. ICP stopped supporting the system in 1987 when they introduced a new system using IDBMS facilities. The system and all changes made to the system, including access to Acme's Local Area Network (LAN), have been designed, developed, and are maintained by Acme's MIS staff. Annual maintenance costs are budgeted at $135,000.*
3. *Internally developing and maintaining a new inventory control system is too costly: $335,000 to develop and with estimated annual maintenance expenses of $55,000.*
4. *Purchasing the Automated Inventory Control System (AICS) from Universal Software presents the best alternative. Purchase price of $150,000 with annual maintenance fees of $22,500 after the first year.*

5. Internally developing and implementing a new inventory control system will take too long to complete: estimated at twelve (12) months.
6. Universal Software's system can be implemented in four (4) months including the design and development of custom reporting requirements.
7. AICS will fully interface with Acme's LAN and current purchasing and accounts payable systems; this will eliminate the need for the three clerical positions.

The Study Team recommends:

1. Acme Manufacturing purchase Universal Software's Automated Inventory Control System (AICS); capital expenditure of $150,000
2. Begin a four (4) month AICS implementation at an estimated total cost of $100,000. (See Section IV: Implementation for details.)

The Study Team estimates cost savings resulting from the implementation of Universal Software's AICS as follows:

Current System Costs:

• *Annual Maintenance:*	*$135,000*
• *Clerical Costs:*	*60,000*
Total	*195,000*

AICS Costs: (based upon a seven-year useful life for the system)

- *Project and Software*
  Depreciation: *$ 35,700*
- *Costs of Funds (8%):*   *6,000*
- *Annual Software*
  Maintenance: *$ 19,300**
- *Annual Maintenance:*   *50,000***
       Total   *110,000*

Total Annual Savings   *$ 85,000*

Years Needed to Payback Project
Investment of $250,000:   *2.94 years*

Increased Earnings per Share: *$0,0115*

   * six years of maintenance fees spread over seven years
** estimated internal AICS maintenance expenses

Section IV: Project (or Implementation) Plans

See Chapter 13, *Section IV: Project or Implementation Plans,* for details.

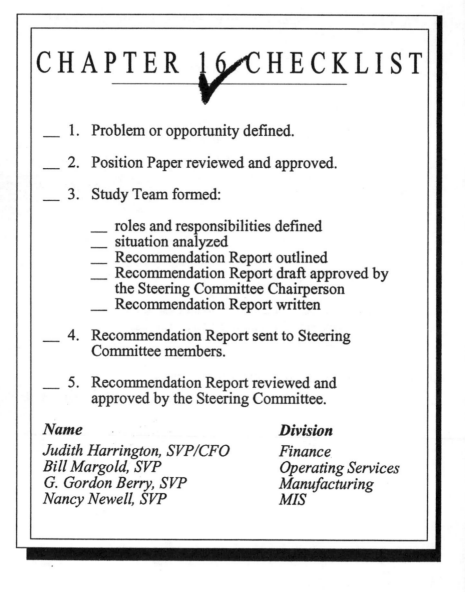

CHAPTER 16 CHECKLIST

___ 1. Problem or opportunity defined.

___ 2. Position Paper reviewed and approved.

___ 3. Study Team formed:

    ___ roles and responsibilities defined
    ___ situation analyzed
    ___ Recommendation Report outlined
    ___ Recommendation Report draft approved by
    the Steering Committee Chairperson
    ___ Recommendation Report written

___ 4. Recommendation Report sent to Steering
    Committee members.

___ 5. Recommendation Report reviewed and
    approved by the Steering Committee.

Name	*Division*
Judith Harrington, SVP/CFO	*Finance*
Bill Margold, SVP	*Operating Services*
G. Gordon Berry, SVP	*Manufacturing*
Nancy Newell, SVP	*MIS*

CHAPTER 17

◆

THE BEGINNING

"We face two options: either renewal and reform or revolution and ruin."

John Diebold
Computer Consultant

The Beginning—Not the End

When we completed this book, we were tempted to say it was finished.
We captured our best ideas and experiences, now on to something else.
In reality, we think this book may be just a small part of the tip of a large
iceberg. We think more sales professionals and organizations are beginning to see that they need to put quality into their selling activities. They
need to create and sustain quality customer service in selling by creating
partnerships with their buyers.

We based this book on the premise that quality in sales requires the
development of a sales partnership and a systematic blending of:

* relationship building
* gaining an in-depth understanding of the buyer's needs, wants, and
  business
* creative problem-solving and solution development

In other words, quality selling reflects a cooperative, collaborative, and consultative relationship between the buyer and seller—a sales *partnership*. We think our BASIC Sales System offers a structure for quality selling. We also believe writing quality proposals provides the "missing link" to buyer or customer-driven sales.

This chapter presents more views on quality and sales. Views that will help forge the future for more effective, creative, and quality sales experiences, creating a partnership to help develop win-win experiences for everyone involved in buying and selling.

Quality Selling — What's That?

As we began to formulate our ideas for this book, we talked to numerous salespeople. Many provided us with support and encouragement. However, others reacted with disinterest, denial, resistance, and a "why bother" attitude. They said:

- "Relationships, our product [service], our reputation, and our price sells — not proposals."
- "I've never needed a proposal — why change now."
- "If the buyer asks for a written proposal, I've lost the deal — someone else has it locked up."
- "I'm only interested in closing deals and making quota not a pretty proposal."

These remarks did not surprise us; we think they reflect lack of awareness for the "total quality" movement in this country. They also reflect the exclusion of sales and marketing functions from most quality improvement processes.

We stated earlier in this book that *selling is customer service*—a service before the buyer becomes a customer. We also think a sales proposal is the first product a company delivers to its new customer. Therefore, when a company begins a campaign to improve the quality of its products or services, it must also begin to improve the quality of its sales processes and proposals. If quality service is customer-driven, then quality selling is buyer-driven.

Some organizations and individuals readily will change their attitudes toward selling and the sales profession. They will change their sales processes and begin to view selling as their first opportunity to provide quality customer service; for example, 3M, Motorola, Hewlett-Packard, Xerox, and Johnson Controls. Others will hold to their current attitudes and continue to deny the need for quality in selling. In many respects, these denial attitudes parallel those of the U.S. automobile industry in the 70's and 80's. An industry that denied the importance foreign manufacturers placed on quality.

The Proposal Close Ratio—A Quality Measure

The *Proposal Close Ratio* provides an excellent measure of the sales process and proposal quality. This ratio compares the number of signed contracts to the number of proposals written. It reflects the effectiveness [doing the right thing] and efficiency [doing the thing the right way] of the selling organization and its sales professionals. The higher the ratio the fewer proposals an organization needs to write to get one signed contract.

In researching this book we found a few companies with Proposal Close Ratios of 50% or higher; however, most had ratios of 20%–30%. Some companies were writing 9–10 proposals to get one deal; their sales forces were not very productive.

We found one division of a Fortune 500 company whose sales manager still thought selling was a numbers game: a sales professional must make 30 calls to get 10 leads and 3 closes. It was not surprising this division used a "boilerplate" proposal approach and had a Proposal Close Ratio of 11%. Each sales professional had a proposal quota of 10 per month. They were always busy finding new leads and generating non-empathetic proposals.

These sales professionals never had enough time to understand their prospective buyer's specific needs and wants. When they lost a deal, price was the most frequently cited reason. Ironically, this company had the best product and customer service in the industry. This division's management needed to make a paradigm shift in their sales processes:

spend more time with each buyer to develop a sales partnership, sell on value not price, write fewer but more buyer-driven proposals [4–6 per month], and close one or two deals per month. More than likely, the Proposal Close Ratio would average 30% or higher.

We also found several companies that taught their sales professionals to sell by providing their buyers business solutions to business problems or opportunities. They used consultative sales processes—first define the problem [or opportunity] and then propose a business solution. It was not surprising to find most of these companies were writing buyer-driven proposals and had the higher than average Proposal Close Ratios.

Changes for the Sales Professional

People will not change if they do not believe in the possibility of a new, more effective sales approach. To most people, change means risk and uncertainty. Often, self-examination helps to avoid negative views before trying something new. As a sales professional, it may be worthwhile to answer the following questions before changing your selling paradigm:

- What particularly strong views do I have that may interfere with my ability to see things from the buyer's point of view?
- What values, perspectives, or prejudices do I have regarding the ideal sales interaction?
- What is more important to me, accomplishing my personal sales and monetary goals or satisfying the needs and wants of my buyers?
- What assumptions am I making that might interfere with my ability to understand and be empathetic to the buyer?

Answering these questions will give you insight into understanding personal attitudes in selling situations. For some, it may even indicate the need to change their attitudes towards customers.

We suggest you also answer these three questions before calling on your next buyer:

- What must I do to develop a sales partnership with this buyer?
- What must I do to understand this buyer's needs or wants?
- What must I do to succeed in helping this buyer solve their business problem?

If you allow your answers to direct their behavior, you may find major changes taking place in your selling activities. You may also see significant changes in your buyer's attitude toward you and your organization.

Leadership is the Key

As mentioned in Chapter 6, the "85/15 Rule" states 85% of an organization's problems [and failures] are the fault of management-controlled systems; workers control less than 15% of the problems. Sales processes and functions are the epitome of management-controlled systems. Therefore, any changes in the way an organization approaches selling must start at the top. It must start with changes in leadership's behaviors and attitude because their behaviors and attitudes set the direction for the entire organization, including the sales staff. We also believe the pathway to developing a sales partnership approach begins with leadership. We think an organization's leadership should answer the following question. Are our organization's sales activities going to become buyer or customer-driven, based on their needs and wants, or will our activities continue to be company-driven, totally based on our quarterly sales quotas and numbers?

Quality Means Honesty and Integrity

Organizations that are customer-driven sell with honesty and integrity. They sell from the top line, not the bottom line. These organizations understand that by satisfying their buyers' needs they also satisfy their own needs. Customer-driven organizations make quality selling their ongoing, top priority. They constantly seek to improve their sales activities, processes, and systems. By improving the way they sell, they:

- constantly improve their sales volume and profits
- build long-term customer relationships—partnerships
- improve the quality, knowledge, and skills of their sales force—raise the level of professionalism
- continually improve their proposals, sales processess, and services and products through customer [buyer] feedback

Continuous Improvement

Organizations committed to quality constantly seek to improve their products and services. Any organization committed to quality must also continually improve its most important customer service function — sales.

Improving the quality of sales means adopting the following changes:

- Make sales customer-driven, not driven by the organization's short-term goals.
- Make everyone in the organization, from top-management to the newest salesperson, obsessed with developing sales partnerships and providing quality service [selling] to their customers.
- Use the Quality Proposal RATER or other feedback instruments to assess the customers' [and buyers'] attitudes about the organization's sales approach and people.
- Review, study, and analyze sales work using quality techniques and team problem-solving methods.
- Make sales education a top priority. Insure salespeople gain and constantly improve their:
  - service or product knowledge
  - knowledge of how and why their services or products provide business solutions for their customers
  - understanding of the critical role they play in delivering quality customer service
  - oral and written communication skills
- Provide salespeople with support, direction, resources, and systems to establish and maintain quality in sales.

- Make selling, including writing proposals, a high-performance team effort with appropriate structures and incentives.
- View selling as the most critical customer service function in the organization, because unless an organization sells, there are no customers to service.
- Put quality into every sales nook and cranny.

It Will Take Forever

Putting quality into selling will not happen overnight. An organization cannot take one big step to reach a quality selling level. It must take many small, and frequently, painful steps. It will require a constancy of purpose. If an organization wants to remain competitive, it must forever look for ways to improve quality. Continuous improvement in sales must become a way of life or a sustained change in the organization's culture, not another short-lived, training program or new sales gimmick.

"Get Ready to Work Hard —

Redirecting an Organization's paths of habit and convenience is very hard work. If senior managers are to assume the mantle of ... leadership, they best be prepared to work at it. Senior managers cannot delegate responsibility for ... quality improvements; they themselves must lead the charge or nothing will happen."

Valerie A. Zeithaml, A. Parasuraman,
& Leonard L. Berry
Delivering Quality Service, The Free Press, 1990

E P I L O G U E

◆

SELLING FROM THE TOP LINE IS
THE BOTTOM LINE

Whether you are a salesperson, sales manager, consultant, or an entrepreneur trying to figure out this game called sales, we believe that selling from the top line will restore sales energy and enthusiasm. Selling with clear purpose and integrity will make a difference to the bottom line.

Quality selling also makes a difference by:

- creating long-term customer relationships
- empowering sales professionals to increase their sense of ownership and responsibility of the sales processes
- giving customers [buyers] what they need and want

While researching and writing this book, we received many helpful suggestions and much support from all levels of sales professionals.

We want to know:

- what works in your proposals
- what you think about our "walking the talk" theory in selling and writing quality proposals
- any creative ways you found to put proposals together
- what are three most important things your customers want from you in your proposals

Write and share your stories and ideas and we will share them in our next book. Of course, we will keep whatever you send us completely confidential.

In conclusion, we are asking you to help us create a new tomorrow in sales. We want this book to become the beginning of a quality revolution in sales. We want our next book to analyze and refine what buyers and [customers] want from consultants and sales professionals.

Bob Kantin
Mark Hardwick
Quality Sales Institute
5956 Sherry Lane, Suite 1000
Dallas, Texas 75225

APPENDIX A

QUALITY PROPOSAL EXAMPLE

This Appendix contains a complete quality proposal example. It is based on a fictitious software and professional services company, PreciseSelect, Incorporated, to a fictitious bank, First State Bank of Texas. Any similarity between these two organizations and actual organizations is purely coincidental.

Note: This proposal makes reference to proposal appendices. These appendices were not included in this example.

FIRST STATE BANK OF TEXAS

A Proposal to

Automate the Teller Selection and Hiring Process

March 11, 1993

PreciseSelect, Incorporated
Austin, Texas

PreciseSelect, Incorporated
1275 North Conway Blvd
Austin, Texas 75012

March 11, 1993

Ms. Doris Quinlin,
Senior Vice President
First State Bank of Texas
1 FSBT Center
Dallas, Texas 75201

Dear Ms. Quinlin:

PreciseSelect, Incorporated (PSI) appreciates the opportunity to submit the enclosed proposal for your review and consideration. We have prepared this proposal in response to your request to present proven methods for reducing First State Bank of Texas' high Teller turnover rate. This high Teller turnover rate has resulted in:

* escalating selection, hiring, and training expenses
* lower customer service levels at the Bank's branches

PSI's industrial psychologists have conducted numerous studies and research projects to determine the causes for employee turnover. Their findings overwhelming pointed to one primary cause — ineffective and inconsistent employee selection and hiring techniques. PSI's Automated Employee and Selection System (AESS) offers a proven solution by using:

* unbiased and validated computer-based selection tests to pre-screen applicants
* computer-based interviews to evaluate applicant responses to critical incident situations

Page 2

Over the past eight years, PSI has implemented AESS in over 100 major corporations. All of these clients realized a payback on their investment in the first six to nine months. These clients continue to use PSI's annual evaluation services to update and re-validate their tests and interview scenarios.

As we agreed, I will present AESS and proposal to your Bank's Senior Management Committee meeting on March 18th at 9:00 a.m. If you have any questions before the meeting, please call me at 1-800-555-TEST.

Thank you again for giving PSI this opportunity. Personally, I would also like to thank you and your staff for taking time from your busy schedules to help me gather the information needed to develop this proposal. I look forward to working with you and your staff in the future.

Sincerely,

Bart L. Roberts
Regional Manager

enclosure

BLR:mf

TABLE OF CONTENTS

TABLE OF CONTENTS (continued)

EXECUTIVE SUMMARY

First State Bank of Texas (FSBT) employs 1,360 part-time and full-time Tellers. With a turnover rate of 29%, FSBT must interview, hire, and educate nearly 400 new Tellers each year at a cost of $6,600 per Teller. Total annual new Teller costs are over $2,640,000. The purpose of this proposal is to show how employee selection testing and computer-aided interviewing can reduce these costs.

PreciseSelect, Incorporated (PSI) proposes FSBT implement its Automated Employee Selection System (AESS). This system contains two components:

Selection Testing
- pre-interview tests delivered on a personal computer
- measures personality traits and attitudes, skills, and general learning and problem-solving abilities

Computer-aided Interviewing
- uses a personal computer to simulate critical work incidents
- provides the Recruiter a method for observing and rating applicant responses

AESS offers FSBT several benefits:

- more effective, efficient, and consistent selection and hiring processes and procedures
- the selection of higher quality and more successful candidates
- reduced employment discrimination liability

PSI's system will save FSBT nearly $340,000 in its first year of operation. PSI's software license and implementation fees are $135,700. FSBT would realize a payback in less than five (5) months.

PSI has used its six-phase methodology to implement AESS in over 100 client sites. This methodology provides a project management approach to:

- develop employee profiles
- design and validate selection tests and interview scenarios
- implement AESS

Preliminary estimates indicate PSI could implement AESS at FSBT in less than five months. Implementation activities could begin in mid-April; the system would be operational by early September.

PSI's fees for the project are:

• AESS license fees	$ 75,000
• implementation fees	50,000
• travel-related expenses	6,000
• sales tax (software only)	4,700
Total fees	$135,700

The annual software maintenance fee, including evaluation and re-validation, is 20% of the current AESS license fee. FSBT would pay $15,000 per year after the first year based on the current license fee.

SECTION I: BACKGROUND INFORMATION

A. FSBT Teller Position Information

First State Bank of Texas (FSBT) employs 1,360 part-time and full-time Tellers in over 189 branch offices. Even though FSBT enjoys an annual Teller turnover rate of 29%, each year the Bank must interview, hire, and educate 394 new Tellers.

All FSBT Tellers must have a High School education and pass the Bank's Math Skills Competency test. Other Teller profile elements may include:

- a college degree
- previous retail sales/customer service experience
- teller experience at another financial institution

B. FSBT Selection and Hiring Processes

The current FSBT selection process follows these seven steps for Tellers hired in metropolitan areas:

1. Applicants complete an application
2. Applications are forwarded to the Human Resources Division
3. A Recruiter reviews the applications and invites suitable applicants to interview
4. A Recruiter interviews selected applicants
5. If the interview is satisfactory, the applicant takes the math skills test
6. If the applicant passes the math skills test, he or she then interviews
with the Branch Manager with the open position(s).
7. The Branch Manager makes the final decision.

The Teller selection, interviewing, and hiring processes at outlying branches do not follow the above steps. Rather, Branch Managers select, interview, and hire their branch's staff.

C. FSBT Teller Selection Costs

FSBT's new Teller selection costs can vary depending upon:

- internal cost accounting methods
- labor market conditions
- annual turnover rates and resulting volumes

Most surveys place the average employment cost for a hourly, clerical employee at $1,500. FSBT's Human Resources Division staff stated this cost estimate is very reasonable for their operation. Therefore, FSBT's total annual employment costs for new Tellers hired into metropolitan area branches are:

- Total number of new Tellers hired annually: 394
- Percentage of Tellers hired for metropolitan branches: 80%
- Total number of new Tellers that go through the
  Human Resources Division's selection process
  (394 x 80%):   315
- Average employment cost per new Teller: $1,500

Total Annual Costs (315 x $1,500) $472,500

D. FSBT Teller Selection Needs

It is impossible to determine FSBT's exact Teller selection needs without a thorough and in-depth job analysis. However, conversations with Human Resources Division staff and our past experience in this area point to several major criteria for employee success on the job:

- cognitive ability
- dependability
- a customer service attitude

The ever-increasing complexity of employment law increases the need for FSBT to standardize its employment process to minimize Equal Employment Liability. The need to standardize the selection process will become more important if civil rights legislation now pending in Congress is passed into law.

E. Purpose of This Proposal

This proposal to First State Bank of Texas has two purposes, to:

- show how the use of employee selection tests and computer-aided interviews can:
  - reduce Teller turnover
  - reduce Teller selection and interview costs
  - improve the overall quality of newly hired Tellers
  - reduce job-employee mismatches
  - minimize Equal Employment liability
- present PreciseSelect, Incorporated's Automated Employee Selection System (AESS)

SECTION II: PSI'S PROPOSED SYSTEM

PreciseSelect, Incorporated (PSI) proposes that First State Bank of Texas (FSBT) implement a new approach to the Teller selection and interview process. The proposed Automated Employee Selection System (AESS) for FSBT's Tellers will contain two components:

* Selection Testing
* Computer-Aided Interviewing

A. Selection Testing

The first system component provides for a pre-interview test delivered on a Personal Computer. PSI will validate the test for FSBT's Teller population to measure:

* personality traits and attitudes
* specific skills
* general learning and problem-solving abilities

FSBT will use the pre-interview test results to:

* provide data for rejecting applicants
* select candidates for personal interviews

B. Computer-Aided Interviewing

The Computer-Aided Interview component provides an additional method by which FSBT can assess new Teller applicants. With the use of a Personal Computer, applicants are placed into an interactive situation which simulates critical work incidents. This component provides the Recruiter with a method for rating applicant responses. It allows the Recruiter to observe intuitive responses to critical work situations.

FSBT will realize the following non-financial benefits through implementation of PSI's Automated Employee Selection System (AESS):

- more effective, efficient, and consistent selection and interview processes and procedures
- the selection of quality candidates
- a higher percentage of successful and satisfied employees
- reduced employment discrimination liability through a statistically validated selection process

See Appendix A for more information on employee selection testing, computer-aided interviewing, and PSI's AESS.

C. Non-financial Benefits

The following table lists specific benefits by AESS component:

PROGRAM COMPONENT	NON-FINANCIAL BENEFITS
Selection Testing	• bases pre-interview selection decisions on unbiased, objective data • uses a pre-determined cutoff score to identify only those applicants best suited for the position • shows EEOC compliance because the test is based upon statistically validated data • provides supporting documentation for selection decisions

C. Non-financial Benefits (continued)

PROGRAM COMPONENT	NON-FINANCIAL BENEFITS
Computer-aided Interviewing	• provides additional unbiases data on which to base hiring decisions • brings consistency and structure to the interview process • improves the effectiveness of the interview process — more successful employee-job matches • provides supporting documentation for hiring decisions — reduced liability

D. Financial Benefits

The use of PSI's Automated Employee Selection System (AESS) will provide financial benefits in several areas:

• Selection and Interview Savings

The use of pre-interview Selection Testing will reduce the number of personal interviews FSBT will need to conduct by an estimated 30% through the:

- elimination of unqualified candidates
- increased quality of candidates interviewed

Based upon our analysis, we determined FSBT interviews five (5) candidates for every one (1) Teller hired. The cost to select, interview, and hire one Teller is $1,500. Therefore, FSBT will reduce its overall costs by 30% or $450 for each Teller hired ($1,500 x 30%) = $450).

FSBT will realize total annual savings of:

- Total number of new Tellers that go through the
  Human Resources Division selection process: 315
- Estimated average employment cost savings
  per Teller: $450

Estimated Total Annual Selection and Interview
Savings (315 Tellers x $450) $141,750

- • Savings from Reduced Turnover

We estimate the use of both Pre-interview Selection Testing and Computer-Aided Interviewing will reduce Teller turnover by 10% for Tellers hired in metropolitan areas. Since the current annual turnover rate is 29%, we estimate through the use of AESS, FSBT will lower this rate to 26%.

Reducing the turnover rate will result in additional savings by decreasing the number of new Tellers the Bank hires each year. As a result, FSBT will lower:

- selection, interviewing, and hiring costs (currently $1,500 per new Teller; projected to decrease to $1,050 with PSI's AESS)
- training costs (estimated by FSBT's Accounting Department at $5,130 per Teller)

By reducing turnover, FSBT will realize total annual savings of:

- Reduced number of new Tellers hired and trained: 32
- Hiring and training cost per new Teller
  ($1,050 + $5,130): $6,180
  Estimated Total Annual Savings from Reduced
  Turnover (32 Tellers x $6,180) $197,760

E. FSBT's Total Savings and Payback

• PSI Fees

The total license and project fees for PreciseSelect's AESS and the implementation project are $135,700. (See Section IV for more details)

• Total FSBT savings:

- Estimated Total Annual Selection and Interview
  Savings: $141,750
- Estimated Total Annual Savings from Reduced
  Turnover: 197,760

Estimated Total Annual Savings: $339,510

• Estimated years to payback:

$$\frac{\$135,700 \text{ PSI Fees}}{\$339,510 \text{ Savings per Year}} = 0.40 \text{ years}$$
or
4.8 months

SECTION III: PSI'S PROJECT MANAGEMENT

The success of a project depends not only on the use of a development methodology but also on the skilled management of the project. PreciseSelect, Incorporated (PSI) uses a project management methodology for on time and within budget development and implementation.

A. Project Management Functions

Project management deals with three aspects of development:

- the *quality* of the tests and scenarios
- the project *schedule*
- the project *budget*

All project activities require a cooperative effort between the First State Bank of Texas (FSBT) and PSI. A benefit of effective project management is timely communication between both organizations. This insures that all activities are the result of agreements based on a clear understanding of each project phase's nature and scope.

B. Quality

Of the three aspects of the project (quality, schedule, budget), quality is the one aspect that remains with the Automated Employee Selection System as long as FSBT uses it. For that reason, PSI pays extraordinary attention to quality, without sacrificing schedule and budget. However, we do recognize that problems can arise in meeting expectations and schedules during a project. If problems do occur, we will work closely with your staff to resolve them in a timely manner.

Since starting the company in 1983, PSI's management has instituted quality standards in its software design and implementation engagements. PSI enjoys an excellent reputation with our past and present clients. Appendix B lists our clients– we readily encourage you to use them as references.

C. Scheduled Project Deliverables

The principal deliverables of the project are the final versions of the selection tests and interview scenarios. PSI produces interim deliverables in each phase, as described in Appendix C. These interim deliverables provide for review of the project's progress and approval of deliverables at various stages of the project.

The following table identifies the phases PSI will use for the FSBT project:

PHASE	PHASE NAME	DELIVERABLE
1	Analysis & Design	Project Definition Document
2	Detail Design	• Test Module Design Documents • Interview Scenario Design Documents
3	Development	• Alpha-tested selection tests and interview scenarios
4	Pilot Testing	Validated test and scenario results
5	Implementation	AESS run reports
6	Operation	Post-project Review Report

D. Project Scheduling

PSI understands FSBT's desire and need to implement new selection and interview processes as soon as possible. PSI's Automated Employee Selection System (AESS) is very stable. This permits the establishment of predictable project schedules. If a scheduling problem does occur during development, PSI will make every effort to minimize its impact on the schedule.

PSI bases the timeframe for the FSBT project on:

- the preliminary review of the proposed tests and interview scenarios
- its development experience
- information gathered during conversations with FSBT staff

Based upon these factors, PSI estimated the scope and depth of the project. Keep in mind that these estimates may require some revision based on the findings of the first project phase.

PSI assumed the following when preparing the schedule:

- Availability of FSBT Staff and Resources

   PSI will need these FSBT staff and resources for the project:

   - Branch Operation Division staff to support Teller job analysis
   - Human Resources Division staff to participate in Teller profiling tasks
   - Tellers for validity testing
   - FSBT's Teller Policy and Procedure Manual

   PSI also requests FSBT designate a Project Coordinator to facilitate communication between our organizations

• Prompt Review and Approval Cycles

PSI assumes that FSBT's project staff will return materials sent for
review and approval within five (5) working days. If FSBT's staff
is not certain that they can provide a five-day turnaround time,
they will need to inform PSI's Project Manager during the first
project phase. This will allow the Project Manager to adjust the
schedule accordingly.

E. Project Budget Management

Adherence to the project's budget is primarily PSI's responsibility.
PSI is responsible for the accuracy of the estimated expenditures of
time and resources required to produce the employee selection tests
and computer-aided interview scenarios for FSBT.

There are circumstances in which PSI may come to FSBT for a
change in budget. If delays or rewrites occur because of FSBT
requested changes, PSI's Project Manager will prepare and send
FSBT's Project Coordinator a Budget Change Notice showing the
nature and scope of the change. PSI will not proceed without FSBT
approval.

Revisions late in the development cycle also require a budget
change. If FSBT's project staff decide during the development phase
that the test questions or interview scenarios are not what they want,
the PSI Project Manager will most likely prepare a Budget Change
Notice before making the changes. PSI records and revises tests and
scenarios based upon review changes identified in the first or second
phase of the project. Later revisions are more expensive and time-
consuming than earlier revisions.

F. Project Status Reports

PSI's Project Manager issues Project Status Reports on a monthly basis or whenever there is a scheduled project status meeting. The purposes for the Project Status Report are:

- to keep FSBT's and PSI's staff and management informed on all aspects of the project
- to officially record completion of phase activities and project milestones

G. Why PSI?

PreciseSelect, Incorporated is the recognized industry leader for automated employee selection and computer-aided interview software. Over the past eight years, PSI's highly-trained staff of industrial psychologists and software technicians have continued to enhance the functionality and efficiency of AESS. PSI enjoys a reputation as the benchmark for quality in the industry.

PSI has implemented its Automated Employee Selection System (AESS) in over 100 Fortune 1000 companies. PSI understands that its clients need expert assistance to implement AESS. As a result of early implementation projects, PSI established its Professional Services Department. These professionals developed a project management methodology that integrates software implementation and employee profile and interview scenario development activities into one project. This integration reduces project development and implementation time and costs.

Annually, PSI hosts the International AESS User Group Meeting. Last year 93 of 112 clients sent representatives to the meeting. Traditionally offering workshops on various employee selection and interviewing topics, this meeting also provides a forum to present new AESS enhancements.

SECTION IV: BUSINESS PROPOSAL

A. Project Assumptions

PreciseSelect, Incorporated (PSI) bases the project's staffing levels, schedule, and estimated fees on the following assumptions:

* New Tellers are the target audience for the Automated Employee Selection System — selection tests and computer-aided interviews.
* The selection tests will contain 65-70 questions.
* The computer-aided interviews will contain 20 critical incident scenarios.
* The project will also develop the following supplementary support materials:
  - Administrator's Guide
  - Interviewer's Manual
* First State Bank of Texas (FSBT) staff will participate on the Project Team with:
  - Human Resources Division and Branch Operations Department staff to assist during the design and testing phases
  - a representative group of Tellers for validation testing

B. PSI Project Staff

PSI will assign the following staff from their Professional Services Department to FSBT's project (see table on the next page):

TITLE	ROLE / RESPONSIBILITIES
Project Manager (Lisa Johnson)	• Primary client contact • Project management • Selection test design review • Computer-aided Interview design review • Pilot Test Plan development • Implementation Plan development • Quality control • Post-installation review
Industrial Psychologist (Bob Meyer)	• Selection test design • Computer-aided Interview design • Validation and testing • Pilot testing
Analyst (Sandy Wilson)	• Technical design • Selection question and computer-aided inteview development • Test development and testing • Validation and testing

(See Appendix D for biographical information on these PSI Professional Services Department staff.)

C. FSBT and PSI Project Staffing Levels

FSBT and PSI will staff phases I through VI of the project as
follows (expressed in % commitment level):

ORGANIZATION	POSITION	PHASES					
		I	II	III	IV	V	VI
FSBT	Project Coordinator	25	25	25	25	25	25
	Human Resources	50	50	15	25	25	10
	Branch Automation	50	50	15	25	25	10
PSI	Project Manager	50	25	25	25	25	25
	Industrial Psychologist	100	100	100	50	50	50
	Analyst #1	0	50	100	100	30	50
	Analyst #2	0	50	100	100	30	50

D. Estimated FSBT Project Schedule

PSI understands FSBT's need to quickly enhance their new Teller selection and interview processes. To accommodate this need, PSI is prepared to begin project activities within 30 days of FSBT's acceptance of this proposal. The following table illustrates our estimated implementation schedule:

PHASE	PHASE NAME/ACTIVITIES	START	STOP
1	Analysis & Design	04-15	05-13
2	Detail Design	05-20	06-12
	• Selection Test Design	05-20	06-06
	• CAI Design	06-06	06-12
3	Development	06-11	07-23
	• Selection Tests	06-11	07-02
	• CAI	06-15	07-23
4	Testing	07-16	08-05
	• Selection Tests	07-16	07-22
	• CAI Tests	07-25	08-05
5	Implementation	07-09	08-26
	• AESS (software)	07-09	07-21
	• Tests	07-29	08-26
	• CAI	08-10	08-26
6	Operation	09-03	

E. PSI's Software License and Project Fees

PSI's fees for the project are:

- Automated Employee Selection System
  Permanent License Fee: $ 75,000.00

- Project Fees:

Phase/Description

1	Analysis and Design:	$ 5,000.00	
2	Detail Design:	10,000.00	
3	Development:	15,000.00	
4	Pilot Testing:	7,500.00	
5	Implementation:	7,500.00	
6	Operation:	5,000.00	
			50,000.00

- Travel-related Expenses*   6,000.00

- Sales Tax (software only) @6.25%   4,687.50

TOTAL $135,687.50

* PSI estimates travel-related expenses for its staff at $6,000 for the project. PSI will invoice FSBT for actual expenses on a monthly basis.

F. Invoice Schedule

PSI will invoice as follows:

- AESS License Fee:
  - One-half (1/2) of the total license when PSI receives the accepted AESS License Agreement from First State Bank of Texas
  - One-half (1/2) of the total license fee upon project completion

- Project Fees:

  - Phases 1 - 3:

    One-half (1/2) of each Phase's fee upon initiation of project activities and one-half (1/2) upon completion of the Phase deliverables.

  - Phases 4 - 6:

    Upon completion of Phase activities and deliverables.

- Travel-related Expenses:

  Travel-related expanses are invoiced at the end of each month

G. Ongoing AESS Maintenance

The annual software maintenance fee, including an on-site evaluation and re-validation process, is 20% of the current AESS license fee.

PSI does not charge maintenance fees for the first year. Based on the current license fee, FSBT would pay $15,000 maintenance beginning with year two.

BIBLIOGRAPHY

Bennis, Warren, *On Becoming a Leader*, Reading, MA, Addison-Wesley Publishing, Inc., 1989.

Crosby, Philip B., *Quality is Free*, New York, McGraw- Hill, 1979.

Deming, W. Edwards, *Out of the Crisis*, Cambridge, MA, Massachusetts Institute of Technology, Tenth Printing, August 1990.

DePree, Max, *Leadership Is an Art*, New York, Dell Publishing, 1989.

Eigen, Lewis D., and Siegel, Johathan P., *The Management Book of Quotations*, Rockville, MD, The Quotation Corporation, 1989.

The Ernst and Young Quality Improvement Group, *Total Quality*, Homewood, IL, Dow Jones-Irwin, 1990.

Excellence Achieved: Customer Service Blueprints For Action From 50 Leading Companies, Waterford, CT, Bureau of Business Practice, Prentice Hall, 1991.

Goldzimer, Linda Silverman, *"I'm First:" Your Customers Message to You*, New York, Rawson Associates, Macmillan Publishing Company, 1989.

Guaspari, John, *The Customer Connection*, New York, AMACOM, a division of American Management Association, 1988.

Hanan, Mack, *Consultative Selling*, New York, AMACOM, a division of American Management Association, 1985.

Holtz, Herman, *The Consultant's Guide to Proposal Writing*, 2nd Edition, New York, NY, John Wiley & Sons, Inc., 1990.

Horn, Robert E., *Mapping Hypertext*, Lexington, MA, The Lexington Institute, 1989.

LeBreuf, Micheal, *How to Win Customers and Keep Them for Life*, New York, Berkley Publishing Group, 1989.

Miller, Robert B., and Heiman, Stephen E., *Strategic Selling*, New York, William Morrow & Company, Inc., 1985.

Peters, Thomas J., *Thriving on Chaos*, New York, Alfred A. Knopf, 1987.

Peters, Thomas J., and Waterman, Jr., Robert H., *In Search of Excellence*, New York, Warner Books, 1984.

Quality Excellence Achieved: Quality Assurance Blueprints For Action From 50 Leading Companies, Waterford, CT, Bureau of Business Practice, Prentice Hall, 1991.

Scholtes, Peter R., *The Team Handbook*, Madison, WI, Joiner Associates, Inc., 1988.

Sewell, Carl, and Brown, Paul B., *Customers for Life*, New York, Doubleday, 1990.

Wilson, Larry, *The Changing Game: The New Way to Sell*, New York, Simon & Schuster, 1988.

Zeithaml, Valerie A., Parasuraman, A., and Berry, Leonard L., *Delivering Quality Service*, New York, The Free Press, A Division of Macmillan, Inc., 1990.

INDEX

HOW TO DEVELOP WINNING SALES PROPOSALS©

A seminar based on the book
"Quality Selling Through Quality Proposals"

As you have discovered in this book, developing the contents and format for a customer-driven, quality sales proposal is a critical success factor for companies involved in complex sales. Research shows that:

- a proposal is the first tangible buyers receive from most sellers; it provides the buyer with valuable insight into the selling organization
- proposals sell long after the sales professional leaves
- the majority of complex sales decisions are made by committees whose members may only read the selling organization's proposal and attend a presentation
- there are no "wired contracts," less than 30 percent of the sellers who are invited to propose have prior relationships with buyers
- buyers select sellers whose proposals communicate:
  - the benefits they would realize from the seller's products or services
  - a detailed understanding of the buyer's specific needs and wants
  - the seller's capabilities and expertise

Further, improving the quality of sales proposals can dramatically improve "Proposal Close Ratios." In some organizations increasing this ratio from 25 to 35 percent can mean a 40 percent increase in revenues.

Most sales training organizations only make cursory mention of proposals in their program offerings. To fill this gap the Quality Sales Institute (QSI), of which this book's co-authors are principals, offers the seminar "How to Develop Winning Sales Proposals©." The objective of this seminar is to provide Sales Managers, Business Development Managers, consultants, and sales professionals with the knowledge, attitudes, and skills to effectively manage and influence the development of winning sales proposals.

For more information on this seminar and other QSI programs and consulting services contact:

Quality Sales Institute
5956 Sherry Lane, Suite 1000
Dallas, Texas 75225
(214) 750-8787

© 1992. All rights reserved. Quality Sales Institute.